INTRODUCTION

Massive golden Mask of the body at the south end of the First Sepulchre, Mycenae. (Reproduced from H. Schliemann, Mycenae: A Narrative of Researches and Discoveries at Mycenae and Tiryns [New York 1878] p. 289)

Heinrich Schliemann is the most famous archaeologist in the world. Support for this extraordinary claim may be found in the many publications about Schliemann that pour from the press more than 100 years after his death. But the strongest evidence is that Schliemann's name is arguably the first, if not the only, name of an archaeologist likely to be recognized by members of the general public. In my conversations with students in introductory archaeology courses, or indeed people in all walks of life, Schliemann is almost always the only archaeologist they can identify by name. His name is on virtually every list of archaeologists, past or present, which is something that cannot be said about anyone else in the field, living or dead.

This continuing fame is surprising because Schliemann's reputation as an archaeologist is currently at an all-time low. But it has not always been thus. Half a century after his death, Schliemann was the major figure in archaeology, and in many publications rather extravagant claims were made about his role as the founder of the discipline or at least the sub-discipline of

Aegean prehistory. In 1939, for instance, Stanley Casson said that Schliemann was "the founder of modern scientific archaeological method and that his work 'constituted an innovation of the first order of importance in the study of the antiquity of man by archaeological methods'" (Daniel 1981, 129). This high encomium was echoed by the popular writer C.W. Ceram who accepted Schliemann's autobiographical accounts without question and described him as a "hero" in the history of archaeology. Ceram claimed that Schliemann was "one of the most astounding personalities not only among archaeologists but among all men to whom any science has ever been indebted" (Ceram 1951, 29), and devoted two long chapters to a sometimes breathless description of his exploits. Ceram's evaluation influenced successive generations of students in archaeology because his book was reprinted many times in the 50 years since it was published. It continued to be used as a textbook in archaeology courses in America well into the 1980s and is still in print today.

Such views were not confined to popular writers like Ceram. Alan Wace, the excavator of Mycenae, asserted that Schliemann had discovered a new world for archaeology and "the greatness of his work is now triumphantly recognized by the majority of learned opinion . . . and his fame as the founder of the science of Aegean archaeology and as the first excavator of the site of Troy is unshakably established" (Wace and Stubbings 1962, 325–26). This opinion was shared by Carl Blegen, one of the preeminent Aegean prehistorians of the 20th century who excavated at Troy in the 1930s. Blegen went on record to say that Schliemann had, by the end of his career, "made himself an experienced, trained, observant excavator who could hold his own with anyone" (Blegen 1963, 27); a statement made in the context of general praise for Schliemann's drive and determination. To still others, Alan Samuel, for example (Samuel 1966, 8), Schliemann was nothing less than "the founder of modern archaeology." And in 1967, William McDonald, himself a pioneer in Aegean prehistory, described Schliemann as "a unique genius...a pioneer who made the decisive breakthrough into Greek prehistory" (McDonald 1967, 9). McDonald's appreciative reassessment of Schliemann's contributions to archaeology (McDonald 1967, 9–13) parallels that given by Blegen, noting Schliemann's originality in his approach to fieldwork, his tendency to investigate the subject in a multidisciplinary manner, his efforts to consult specialist colleagues, and his "passionate desire to get at the truth from every possible angle [which] shines out clearly."

ACKNOWLEDGEMENTS

17 MARCH 2006

I wish to thank Maria Pilali and the librarians of the Gennadius and Blegen libraries of the American School of Classical Studies at Athens for their assistance. It is a pleasure to acknowledge also the help provided by Katherine Kominis at the Gotlieb Center for Archival Research at Boston University and Staley Ellis Cushing at the Boston Athenaeum.

I have made great use of David Traill's biography of Heinrich Schliemann, which is a gold mine of information. Traill's biography is a monumental scholarly accomplishment and the starting point for any research on the life and work of Schliemann. Although professor Traill's focus was not on Schliemann's archaeological publications, he provides a great deal of incidental detail of value to bibliographers and bibliophiles alike.

My greatest debt is to Professor George Styl. Korres, professor of Archaeology Emeritus of the University of Athens. His many scholarly works on Schliemann form one of the richest sources of information based on firsthand inspection of the Schliemann archive in Athens. As the testimony of these pages makes clear, I could not have written this handlist without Korres's work, which includes the first, the best, and the only comprehensive bibliography of printed works pertaining to Heinrich Schliemann. Professor Korres provided me with a copy of his bibliography, which is very hard to obtain today outside of Greece, and his kindness was especially valuable because the copy he provided was corrected and updated in his own hand. It is a great pleasure to acknowledge professor Korres's collegial support and great kindness, and it is indeed difficult to express adequately in mere words my gratitude for his thoughtful generosity, which is intertwined with a profound respect for his great industry and careful scholarship.

Professor William M. Calder III very kindly offered his views of the first edition of this book, and his useful, interesting, and welcome suggestions for clarifications and corrections were taken into consideration in the preparation of this new edition of the handlist. I appreciated both the gift of numerous offprints and books, and the collegial and lively correspondence that ensued.

Mark Kurtz, Marni Blake, and Kevin Mullen of the Archaeological institute of America warmly supported this project from a very early stage, and helped produce the present book, bringing to bear their professional expertise on every facet of its production, from the design of the cover to the eBook edition.

Al B. Wesolowsky, long-time friend and confident, kindly agreed to read the manuscript of the first edition, and I wish to thank him for his many helpful and judicious suggestions for improvements, both large and small. I hope he will forgive me for not making all of the corrections that he suggested. Finally, it is a great pleasure to acknowledge the help that Priscilla Murray provided. We have frequently discussed the handlist from its inception in 2001, and she has assisted with editing making many useful comments about matters both large and small that I have taken to heart, whether she knows it or not.

finally, Glyn Daniel, the historian of archaeology, described Schliemann simply, and without qualification, as the founder of Greek archaeology who inspired a generation of archaeologists (Daniel 1950, 136–41).

As I noted above, Schliemann's reputation has declined in recent years, and today Schliemann is no longer praised in an unqualified way. In histories of archaeology written at the end of the 20th century he is sadly ignored (e.g., Schnapp 1996), or, as in the writings of Bruce Trigger, receives a bare two sentences in a book of 500 pages on the history of archaeology, where he is acknowledged merely as one who "pioneered the stratigraphic excavation of multi-layered 'tell' sites" (Trigger 1989, 197). Not all writers take such a dismissive view. J. Lesley Fitton, for instance, has a long and very interesting chapter on Schliemann's work at Troy and Mycenae (Fitton 1995, 48–103) acknowledging Schliemann as "one of the most famous names in archaeology" and describing his finds at Troy and on the Greek mainland as the "most dramatic and significant ever made by any individual," concluding that Schliemann was "without doubt one of the discipline's most remarkable pioneers" (Fitton 1995, 54). It is hard to argue with this conclusion. Hedged about with the appropriate qualifications ("one of the most," "arguably," "one of the discipline's"), these statements represent, one would think, the general run of opinion of the historians of archaeology today.

The decline in Schliemann's reputation in the last 25 years is in part the result of renewed study of Schliemann's archaeological activities occasioned by the centennials of Schliemann's first excavations at Troy, his discovery of the Shaft grave circle at Mycenae, and his death in 1890 (Calder 1972; Traill 1993). These occasions were opportunities for a wide range of new studies of Schliemann and his work. Arguably the most significant of the publications that have resulted is the biography by David Traill (Traill 1995), which presents the best and most fully documented account of Schliemann's life (Runnels 1997). Traill's biography is an in-depth, detailed study of Schliemann's life in all of its complexity, and is part of an intensive scholarly enterprise that has spanned decades and involved many people (Calder 1972; Calder and Traill 1986; Traill 1993). Traill's biography represents a significant departure from earlier accounts that relied heavily and uncritically on Schliemann's autobiographical writings. Earlier biographies (e.g., Ludwig 1931; Payne 1959) tended to hagiography and relied on Schliemann's autobiographical writings, but Traill's biography is based on a thorough firsthand study of primary documentary sources, particularly the letters, diaries, and other unpublished materials found in collections such as the archive of Schliemann papers found in the Gennadius library in Athens. Other biographies are helping to throw light on Schliemann's archaeological career, for instance, Susan Heuck Allen's biography of Frank Clavert, who introduced Schliemann to the site of Hisarlik (Allen 1999). Although Allen limited her review of Schliemann's life and work to those aspects that overlapped with her study of the contribution made by Frank Clavert to the discovery of Troy, she carefully reviewed the available material that related to Schliemann and has added to the evolving picture of Schliemann's beginnings in archaeology.

The ever-widening circle of new and widely available scholarship on Schliemann published in this period of revision has produced some decidedly negative discoveries concerning his veracity and standards of personal conduct (e.g., von Burg 1987; Calder 1972; Calder and Traill 1986). Despite the wide publicity surrounding some of the revelations and accusations made about Schliemann, the new wave of scholarship has also led to a sometimes grudging appreciation of Schliemann's positive contributions to archaeology. Schliemann was perhaps a better archaeologist than some critics have admitted. When I was a student in the 1960s and 1970s, Schliemann was often a byword in bad archaeology. He appeared in textbooks as a ham-handed gold-seeker who destroyed the sites he excavated. "Old Schliemann," we were told, was an old-fashioned treasure hunter who contributed nothing to archaeology. Denying that Schliemann was the "father of Archaeology" (as he was sometimes called) was a mark of sophistication and learning among aspiring archaeologists in the second half of the 20th century. This was not the universal opinion, of course, and Schliemann continued to receive respectful attention from some (e.g., Daniel 1967), but there was truth in the assertion that Schliemann had been overrated as an archaeologist in his lifetime and the decades immediately after his death. Despite the sometimes negative findings, the recent scholarship may yet do something to restore some of Schliemann's reputation as an archaeologist. It is hardly to be disputed that he learned his craft rapidly and in the course of his archaeological career changed from an enthusiastic but careless amateur (Allen 1999) into a seasoned and innovative professional (Korres 1990, 48–50; Runnels 1997; Trigger 1989, 197) who may regain a place as one of the founders of modern field archaeology. More than Trigger's "pioneer…[of the] stratigraphic excavation of multi-layered 'tell' sites," Schliemann's contributions to archaeology include the use of trial trenches, the practice of extensive stratified excavation, the use of pottery for relative and absolute dating, the practice of making trial excavations to establish negative evidence, and the use of the comparative method with an emphasis on the close examination and classification of all classes of artifacts in addition to architectural and stratigraphic features (Witte 1990). Witte also observes, correctly in my opinion, that Schliemann was a pioneer in what we would today call "multidisciplinary" approaches to archaeology. He took an interest in technology, geography, geology, cartography, meteorology, ethnology, anthropology, botany, photography, and technical analyses of metal, which can be seen, to take one but example, in the many appendices to *Ilios* (1880c). Particularly significant is Schliemann's clear understanding that an archaeological site could not be understood in isolation from its hinterland or geographic location in a territory (Witte 1990, 47). This appreciation of the site in its countryside can be seen in his earliest work (*Ithaque*, 1869) and is clearly developed in his mature works (e.g., *Ilios, Troja, Reise*). Above all, Schliemann excelled his contemporaries and most modern archaeologists in his rapid publication of his excavations (Korres 1990). His publishing record has rarely been matched, much less surpassed by modern archaeologists, much to their shame. For his excavations at Troy, Mycenae, Orchomenos, and Tiryns he published illustrated monographs within a year of completing his excavations, sometimes, as can be seen from the list below, from as many as five different publishers in four different languages on two continents. No one is perfect, and as Korres (1990) noted, Schliemann left many artifacts and other remains from his main excavations unpublished, as he did also with most of the material from his smaller excavations (e.g., at Paleokastro and the Cave of Nestor in Messenia, Motye in Sicily, Kythera, Thermopylae, and the Tomb of the Athenians at Marathon). What is remarkable is that these omissions were the exceptions to his rule of rapid and relatively complete publication.

If Schliemann's abilities as an archaeologist are perhaps better than we thought, we can nevertheless have no illusions about the virtues of Schliemann's public or private life. He was a pioneer and not a saint. Ever since the groundbreaking research of Calder and Traill first brought to light details of Schliemann's life and work based on the careful study of the archival documents, opinions on Schliemann as a man and an archaeologist have shifted (Calder and Traill 1986 offer a good selection of these studies).

It is clear that much of what has been written or said about Schliemann in the last century is in need of serious revision. Schliemann was a complex man whose life and work is only now coming under close examination. It is increasingly clear that some of his ethical failings may require changes in our understanding of his contributions to prehistoric archaeology and Aegean prehistory. We may have perhaps become too critical, and if we do not believe the old biographies and have come to doubt much of the veracity of Schliemann's autobiographical writings, some of the more shocking claims about Schliemann's unethical archaeological behavior such as the salting of sites with artifacts and the faking of antiquities (e.g., Traill 1995) are themselves in need of more research before they can be accepted uncritically (Runnels 1997). The details of Schliemann's life and work are likely to be debated for a very long time; in this short work I do not wish to contribute to the debate over Schliemann's personal or business activities, nor is this essay and handlist a contribution to the biographical literature on Schliemann. My aim is to contribute to the study of Schliemann's archaeological achievements by providing a comprehensive list of his published works on the prehistoric archaeology of the Aegean world.

For any assessment of the man and his work, full documentation of his publications is essential, and there has long been a need for a comprehensive list in English of his archaeological publications. After more than 100 years, the bibliographic details of the world's best known archaeologist are found scattered among biographical studies, collections of letters, research library catalogues, antiquarian booksellers' lists, and exhibition catalogues. These works are in many languages, oftentimes out of print, and always hard to find. Furthermore, the lists I have consulted are incomplete, contradictory, and sometimes clearly inaccurate. Archaeologists, like booksellers, have a tendency to transcribe or transfer bibliographic references from other publications to their bibliographies rather than examining the cited works firsthand. As a consequence, confusion and misinformation awaits the unwary scholar who consults the available lists of Schliemann's publications in libraries or the catalogues of antiquarian book dealers. An example that comes readily to mind is the confusion in the dating of the second (or "New") US edition of *Mycenae* with a title having the date of 1880, or 1881, or sometimes no date at all.

The only complete bibliography of which I am aware of writings by and about the life and work of Heinrich Schliemann was published in Athens by professor George Korres over 25 years ago (Korres 1974). Unfortunately, this book is out of print and, even worse, has never been translated. This is a pity. Professor Korres's bibliography was carried out on an unparalleled scale and includes all, or nearly all, of the newspaper articles, reviews, letters, journal articles, and books written by Heinrich and Sophia Schliemann along with a large number of book reviews, articles, and books written about the Schliemanns by others. In order to compile his bibliography, professor Korres made full use of the many Schliemann papers available in Athenian libraries, particularly the Gennadius library of the American School of classical Studies at Athens. He had access to the extremely large number of books and other materials of the Schliemann family deposited by their children and grandchildren in these institutions. Korres' bibliography includes all of Schliemann's major publications, either books or offprints, and much material from scrapbooks, dossiers with newspaper clippings, reviews, and copies of ephemeral publications by the Schliemanns. These rich sources were thoroughly examined and there is no doubt that Korres's bibliography is the best existing source of information on Schliemann's publications available in any language. In addition to Schliemann's works, professor Korres's bibliography has substantial sections listing the publications of other scholars on topics connected with Schliemann and the sites he investigated. Especially valuable are the lists of contemporary reviews of Schliemann's publications in newspapers, magazines, and journals, and the lists of reprints of Schliemann's publications.

Apart from this important exception, complete bibliographies of Schliemann's work are unavailable. At least in English language publications, Schliemann's writings are cited (e.g., Calder 1972; Traill 1993, 1995), but the bibliographic lists I have examined cannot be accurately described as comprehensive. To be fair, scholars preparing bibliographies for other purposes do not have the same objectives as those who would attempt to compile a specialized bibliography for a single author.

The published bibliographies that I have consulted contain errors, and such lapses in accuracy are not trivial because the errors have a tendency to be copied, and thus perpetuated, in the scholarly and popular literature on Schliemann. As I hope will become clear in this handlist, an accurate ordering and description of Schliemann's published works can contribute to the larger understanding of his contribution to the prehistoric archaeology of the Aegean. Succinctly stated, this handlist is a contribution to the primary documentation of the archaeological career of Heinrich Schliemann. In addition to providing a listing of Schliemann's works, this handlist has been annotated, and it is my hope that these annotations will be of some use to readers who may not be familiar with Schliemann or his work.

I hope that this handlist will be of interest to a wide range of readers. Aegean prehistorians who have a professional need to consult the original works of the founder of their discipline will find it especially useful. After all, Schliemann's original excavation reports are still a vital source of information today on the stratification, architecture, and material culture of the most important sites in the region where excavation and study continue. Schliemann's original publications will always be a starting point for the Aegean prehistorian.

The handlist will also be useful for those writing the history of archaeology. The handlist organizes the various editions of Schliemann's publications in their order of appearance. These details will be useful for the correct cataloguing and description of Schliemann's books, and future biographers of Schliemann may find this handlist useful for evidence of Schliemann's evolution from dilettante to professional archaeologist.

Perhaps the greatest use of the handlist will be made by archaeology students. Aegean prehistory is today a subfield of prehistoric archaeology with practitioners in scores of countries. For this reason a complete list of Schliemann's works is especially necessary. The author recalls his own frustration as a student in attempting to sort out the sometimes similar titles in an effort to distinguish one work from another and to study them in their proper order. To take one example: is Schliemann's book *Mycenae and Tiryns* as it is called in the London and New York editions the same text as *Mycènes* in the French edition (1879), which does not refer to Tiryns in the title, or the later American publication with the title *Tiryns* (1885a)? The answer to such a question may seem obvious to anyone looking at the descriptions available in this book, or who is already familiar with Schliemann's publications, but to a student puzzling over a library computer screen such tricky questions can lead to confusion, wasted time, and frustration.

Librarians will find this handlist helpful in checking bibliographic records and assisting in the proper cataloguing of library holdings, and antiquarian booksellers, collectors, and bibliophiles of all stripes will find the handlist an essential tool for the collation and correct identification of different editions and translations. Finally, many general readers will find in a complete listing of Schliemann's writings many curious facts of intrinsic interest concerning the history of his explorations and excavations that may repay them for the time spent in perusing these pages.

As a result of preparing the first edition of this book, I noticed that booksellers' and librarians' descriptions of Schliemann's published works tend often to be inaccurate, the result I believe of copying descriptions of books directly from other catalogues. In an effort to revise the handlist, therefore, I endeavored to acquire copies of as many of these books as possible to enable me to examine the accuracy of the descriptions and wherever possible to examine copies of those works not in my own collection that can be found in libraries. I have noted those instances where it was not possible for me to examine a copy of a particular title firsthand.

PRELIMINARY REMARKS

Map of Argolis. (Reproduced from H. Schliemann, Mycenae: A Narrative of Researches and Discoveries at Mycenae and Tiryns [New York 1878] p. 1)

The following annotated handlist is chiefly concerned with Schliemann's books and selected articles in scholarly journals and omits ephemeral newspaper and magazine articles along with the writings of Sophia Schliemann (all of which can be found in Korres 1974). There are good reasons for confining this handlist to Schliemann's books. For one, professor Korres has compiled a comprehensive bibliography with all of the newspaper articles, reviews, and letters printed in Schliemann's lifetime (Korres 1974). And for another, the content of the publications that are omitted is for the most part no more than one or two printed pages with information, which was often included in Schliemann's books. Only specialists are likely to have any serious interest in reading the newspaper and periodical articles today. Schliemann published, for example, at least 28 newspaper articles on his excavations at Troy (Korres 1974, 7–9) in German, Greek, French, and English in the interval between his first excavation at Troy in 1870 and the publication in 1874 of *Trojanische Alterthümer*. Although the *Augsburger Allgemeine Zeitung* was clearly a favored venue, these articles were published in an impressive array of newspapers and journals ranging from *The Levant Herald* and the *Revue Archéologique* to the *Greek philological Society of Constantinople*. Schliemann typically wrote 10 or 12 of these articles a year. *Trojanische Alterthümer* incorporated most of these reports in its text and this book clearly supersedes those preliminary reports. As a consequence, it seems superfluous to list them again here. This practice of preceding his major publications with a string of ephemeral letters, reports, and articles persisted throughout Schliemann's career. Most of the text of *Mycenae* (1878a), to take another example, was serialized in *The Times of London* before publication in book form by John Murray (Traill 1995, 165). Schliemann probably favored this method of publication because it helped to create interest in the book while it was being written and boosted sales of the finished product. As a result, the ephemeral publications are very numerous indeed, as can be seen in professor Korres's bibliography where more than 220 articles are listed that appeared between 1870 and Schliemann's death in 1890 (including an interesting grouping of the 20 or so telegrams Schliemann sent to the Greek press during his excavations at Mycenae, which includes the famous telegram addressed to George, King of the Hellenes).

The present handlist also does not include the many books, journal articles, encyclopedia articles, and reviews of Schliemann and his works that have been published since Schliemann's death. Professor Korres lists more than 2,000 of these, and since 1974 when he published his bibliography, there has been a sharp increase in the number of publications on Schliemann that would make any comprehensive bibliography very difficult indeed. For those readers who wish to sample this fare I have included posthumous titles such as the publication of Schliemann's letters (e.g., Duell 1977; Lilly 1961) and his American diaries (e.g., Weber 1942). Schliemann's autobiography, however, is a major exception to this rule. Published in 1892 by Sophia Schliemann, the bulk of this text was written at different times by Schliemann himself, and it seems to mark the natural end of any bibliography of his works. Another important non-archaeological book that is included is Schliemann's first book, *La Chine* (1867), which has nothing to do with archaeology and throws no light on Schliemann's later archaeological career. It was his first book, however, and it seems only fitting that this handlist should begin with it, just as it ends with his posthumous *Selbstbiographie*. Although I have chosen to omit most of the periodical literature, a few special examples are included. The articles chosen for inclusion were more than two or three printed pages in length, presented significant archaeological finds, or were in some other way of particular interest.

For most of the works, I have endeavored to include all editions insofar as these could be ascertained, at least those that I was able to examine personally. Additional research would no doubt bring to light more information and enlarge the sphere of detail, but the essential elements are here. Among other sources of information, I have reviewed numerous antiquarian booksellers' catalogues from the 1980s to the time of writing (summer 2005) in order to get a sense of the availability of Schliemann's books, and I have availed myself of the resources of the Gennadius and Blegen libraries at the American School of classical Studies at Athens, the library of the British School at Athens, the Gotlieb Archival Research center at Boston University, the Boston Athenaeum, and the Boston public library (Research library). Where it has not been possible to inspect a book personally, I have relied upon professor Korres's 1974 bibliography, which I have found to be both accurate and reliable in all particulars.

The publications have been listed chronologically; as this is the most convenient way to arrange such diverse materials (an alphabetical short title list at the end of this book is a helpful finding guide). Besides providing an easily comprehended structure for the list, a chronological arrangement reveals the historical progression of Schliemann's travels and archaeological excavations. By viewing his monographs in this way, one can see at a glance how Schliemann's activities changed through time, and one can follow the evolution of the excavation reports, which grow more professional with time, even as they became larger, thicker, more profusely illustrated, and elaborately decorated.

There is much food for thought, I think, in examining Schliemann's lifework from this perspective. Schliemann had a habit of rewriting his own life story, as one can readily see from reading his autobiographical writings, and the problems with this practice have been made abundantly clear by the research of scholars such as Calder and Traill.

An independent source of information for Schliemann's life and archaeological research is needed, and in this handlist one can perceive in the progressive enlargements and refinements in his major publications the development of Schliemann's self-perception as an archaeologist. In his first publications his self-image is that of the world traveler. *La Chine* (1867) and *Ithaque* (1869a), it would seem, were written in French and aimed squarely at the salons of Paris and at the educated classes of Europe in general who read travel literature for pleasure with the rather transparent goal of establishing Schliemann's reputation as a literary person. Only after his conversion to archaeology, which appears to have occurred during his 1868 journey in Greece, did Schliemann begin his metamorphosis into the professional archaeologist.

This transformation can be seen clearly in the sequence of publications, which began in 1874 with *Trojanische Alterthümer* and its English version *Troy and its Remains*. These books are poorly illustrated, haphazardly organized, and improperly documented by today's standards. They are the works of a rank amateur. Schliemann's enthusiasm, wild fantasy, and patent self-aggrandizement leap off of every page. The professional scholars of the European and American academies must have found it difficult to contain their smiles while perusing these works, despite the manifest interest in the exploration of the Troad and the search for Troy. Only four years later, however, Schliemann's publication of his research at Mycenae, although still heavily colored by his amateurish enthusiasm, is both professional in tone, thoroughly illustrated, well documented, and carefully organized. *Mycenae* (1878a) begins to approach the form of a proper excavation report. This trend continued when Schliemann returned to his excavations at Troy after 1878, and the publication of *Ilios* (1880b) signals a new maturity. In this work Schliemann began to incorporate the contributions of specialist scholars of established reputations and included numerous technical appendices of the kind normally found in the best excavation reports of any age. *Ilios* bristles with plans, maps, and countless illustrations of artifacts, skillfully marshaled by Schliemann in an attempt to persuade his skeptical readers of his professionalism and the significance of his discoveries. The documentation in *Ilios* makes it clear that in the interval between 1869 with the publication of *Ithaque* and the publication of *Ilios* in 1880, Schliemann's transformation from dilettante to professional archaeologist had been completed. If nothing else, Schliemann quickly learned the forms and trappings of his chosen profession and abandoned his earlier persona as romantic traveler in order to focus all of his powers of persuasion in an effort to convince readers that he was now a consummate professional.

The transformation from amateur to professional can be seen when one views these books as artifacts. Arrayed on a shelf, a clear progression in size is evident as the books increase from 17 to 26 cm in height (measured from the top to the bottom of the text block; bindings are even larger!); from 221 pages to 800 pages of text; from 4 illustrations to 1,800 illustrations; and from plain cloth to the highly decorative, indeed one may say splendid, gilt blue, red, and gold pictorial cloth used by Schliemann's publishers for his later archaeological works.

The culmination of this trend is surely Schliemann's best work, *Tiryns*, published in 1885. Here we see Schliemann at his professional peak. The high quality of description and illustration in this work, along with the meticulous attention to detail, has suggested to many people that Schliemann's transformation from dilettante to archaeologist was the result of his association with Wilhelm Dörpfeld. The growing professionalism evident in Schliemann's books from 1874 to 1878 however suggests otherwise and his choice of Dörpfeld as a colleague may be rather a *consequence* than a *cause* of this change. *Tiryns* is without doubt the largest and most brilliantly illustrated of all of Schliemann's publications, and in my opinion it is also the best organized, most fully documented, and most mature scholarly work to come from Schliemann's pen. Today it is also the most readable of Schliemann's works because of the clarity of its descriptions, its attention to detail, and its elaborate illustrations. *Tiryns* could serve today as a model of what a good excavation report ought to be. We have in his books, then, the reflection of Schliemann's odyssey from a peripatetic and derivative travel writer of the 19th century to an independent scientist in modern terms.

An indication of the availability of each title in the handlist is noted. Any estimate of availability can be nothing more than a guess based on the citation of copies in the National union catalogue, a publication of the library of congress that lists the holdings of principal libraries, *WorldCat*, a collective on-line bibliographic resource available by subscription, and the frequency with which Schliemann's books appear on the antiquarian book market. The availability of Schliemann's books on the antiquarian book market can be estimated from the catalogues of major dealers, something I have done for a period of about 10 years (1995 to 2005), supplemented by internet trade sites. For the purpose of giving a general impression of the survival, popularity, and availability of Schliemann's books, I examined two sites on the internet: Abe-books (http://www.abebooks.com, accessed 21 December 2001) and Addall (http://www.addall.com, accessed 8 August 2005). These are commercial sites, the former a single site and the latter a site where the user may view the contents of many commercial sites in the united

States and Europe. The following table lists the results of these searches.

Title	Catalogues	AbeBooks	AddALL
La Chine	0	0	0
Ithaque/Ithaka	0	1	2
Trojanische Alterthümer	1	1	0
Atlas	1	0	0
Troy and its Remains	3	5	7
Mycenae/Mycènes/ Mycenae	10	12	27
Ilios	8	10	22
Troja	4	6	16
Tiryns/Tirynthe	7	13	36
Orchomenos	1	0	1
Reise in der Troas	1	0	2

This table reveals that some titles are readily and consistently available on the market while others appear only rarely. No copy of *La Chine et le Japon*, for instance, seems ever to reach the market, while copies of *Mycenae, Ilios, Troja*, and *Tiryns* are always available. Of these, the English language editions, taking US and UK editions together, are the most frequently encountered, typically at the rate of two or three times as often as the French and German editions. The numbers in this table reflect, in my opinion, both the popularity of a title and the numbers of copies printed. In my experience, holdings for major libraries have the same composition as seen in this table.

I conclude that Schliemann's earliest publications, particularly his first publications on Troy and rarer titles, e.g. *Orchomenos*, were issued in very small editions and were not commercial successes. A rather interesting conclusion to emerge is that despite our contemporary tendency to regard Schliemann chiefly as the discoverer of Troy (hence the titles of the two best biographies of Schliemann by Ludwig and Traill: *Schliemann of Troy*), it was in fact his discovery of the Shaft grave circle at Mycenae and the description of these exciting materials in the very popular and successful book *Mycenae* that had the greatest impact. From the foregoing, the argument could be made that Schliemann recognized the amateurish nature of his first publications, at least implicitly, which he did not bother to update or reprint. It was the work of his growing maturity as a field archaeologist that he made available to the public and his colleagues both. These were beautiful, imposing, authoritative books printed in large numbers and widely distributed, underscoring Schliemann's confidence in his powers.

Mycenae was the first of Schliemann's books to be brought out on a grand scale, and it was intended to secure Schliemann's fame in the public eye. As scholars of 19th century publication practices have noted, books like *Mycenae* were a major source of entertainment in Europe and America in the age before radio, cinema, and television. Their imposing physical size, colorful decorated covers, and heavily illustrated texts conveyed an air of adventure and exciting discovery carefully crafted to appeal to the widest possible audience (see David and Saperstein 1996 and Secord 2000, 9–76 *et passim* for a discussion of books as entertainment in Victorian times). Schliemann recognized this and spared no expense in creating a series of books that was calculated to appeal to the largest possible number of readers in order to marshal public support for his discoveries and to silence his critics. The theme of Schliemann's precocious use of the popular media to promote his archaeological career is discussed in further detail in the annotations to the handlist.

TERMINOLOGY

Finally, a word must be said concerning the terminology employed in the annotations. From the earliest days of printing until the first half of the 19th century, publishers and booksellers distributed the printed sheets of a new book in a temporary wrapper, which was almost always replaced with a fine binding by the purchaser of the book, often in rich materials such as leather, vellum, and marbled paper-covered boards. Before the 19th century, the temporary wrappings were themselves made from these materials but in the 18th century thick paper-covered cardboard bindings became the norm. By the 19th century, publishers were in the habit of using a variety of materials for temporary covers. A paper wrapper (like a paperback today) decorated with a printed title and pictorial designs, was one of the most popular materials. By the middle of the 19th century, however, a new method of binding new books was introduced. Pasteboards covered with a thin layer of cloth and called "publisher's cloth" could be embossed or stamped with titles and pictorial designs highlighted with gold or bright colors. These bindings, originally temporary, evolved into what is today called a "hardback." in the Victorian period publishers decorated publisher's cloth, and in time purchasers began to leave these "temporary" bindings on the book rather than replacing them, and as a consequence, bindings became progressively sturdier and more highly decorated. Decorated publishers' cloth bindings consist of two boards, one in front and one in back ("covers"). The "front cover," therefore, is the "upper board" as it is described in most specialized booksellers' catalogues, and the "back cover" is the "lower board" of the catalogues. Schliemann's books as they are offered on the book market and found in libraries today are often bound in fine leather, but the descriptions found in this handlist refer only to the original bindings of publisher's cloth where this can be ascertained.

Booksellers, collectors, publishers, and bibliophiles refer to the size and shape of a book by means of a sort of shorthand. A quarto (4to) is a large square book (the term derives from the practice of folding large printed sheets to form the leaves or pages of the book; two folds resulted in four pages when the edges were sliced open, hence "quarto"). This is the largest format among the Schliemann titles and is typically 26 cm tall (or more) and about 19 cm wide. An octavo (8vo) is smaller and rectangular, about 24 cm by 16 cm. An octavo originally resulted from folding the printed sheet yet again before slicing open the edges to form the pages encountered in the finished text block. A smaller trim size is described here as a 12mo (pronounced "twelvemo" or "duodecimo" in the language of the bibliographer, again describing the practice of folding printed sheets). The abbreviation 12mo refers to a small book typically less than 24 cm tall, although 12mo is not a standardized term when used to describe books published in Victorian times. There is yet a smaller trim size, called a 16mo (pronounced "sixteenmo"). Sixteenmos and twelvemos these days are terms applied to any very small book. The overall size of Schliemann's books shows a great deal of variation, and an exact typology is not possible or necessary. I have relied on the description of the book in catalogues, an examination of the number of leaves per signature (there are four numbered leaves, e.g., D1, D2, D3, D4, in a quarto and eight in an octavo), and taken my own counsel in regarding the size and shape of the book in making my final designation. Whenever in doubt, I have relied upon Korres's 1974 bibliography.

THE HANDLIST
OF THE PUBLISHED WORKS OF HEINRICH
SCHLIEMANN

**Gold buttons from Sepulchre I V, Mycenae. Nos. 402–413. (Reproduced
from H. Schliemann, Mycenae: A Narrative of Researches and
Discoveries at Mycenae and Tiryns [New York 1878] p. 264)**

BOOKS

1867. *La Chine et le Japon au temps présent*. Paris: Librairie Centrale (24,
Boulevard des Italiens). 221 [Korres gives 223 + 2] pp. 12mo. 17.5 cm.
The binding or wrapper issued with the book has not been determined.

This was Schliemann's first major publication. It is a description in the
form of a diary of a trip undertaken from May to September, 1865, as part of
Schliemann's journey around the world in that year. It makes no mention of
his ambition to be an archaeologist or to search for the remains of Homeric
Troy. This failure to note his "life-long interest in Troy," which is elsewhere
related in romantic detail in his autobiographical writings, supports the view
of those who believe that his interest in archaeology did not take shape until
after his first trip to Greece in 1868 (Traill 1995). If Schliemann had not
become famous as an archaeologist, this book would have done nothing to

secure his fame. It is dull. Not a single map or illustration relieves the tedium. The descriptions of the Great Wall of China, Tokyo, and Kyoto are entirely conventional and nowhere rise above those found in the travel literature at the time. Compared with the plethora of sophisticated travel books from the 19th century (here one thinks of Kinglake's *Eothen*, or, perhaps closer to the topic, the works of Lafcadio Hearn on Japan), *La Chine* fails to measure up. To the modern reader and the student of Schliemann, perhaps the most curious feature of the book is Schliemann's habit of mentioning the exact amount paid for goods and services. Schliemann, ever the shopkeeper, is fascinated with the prices of things, even the most trifling sums. One sees this tendency still in his archaeological writings. In *Tiryns* (p. 4) he positively crows, for instance, over the measly 10 Greek lepta (about two US cents at the time) that he paid for "a cup of black coffee, without sugar" in Nafplion's Agamemnon café. Part of the fascination of his character is found in such eccentricities. Why does an immensely wealthy man find it necessary to inform the reader of an otherwise learned archaeological tome of how little he managed to pay for his coffee?

The print run of *La Chine* was probably quite small. I suspect that a few hundred copies (fewer than 500 would be a good guess) were printed at his own expense; these would have been given away by Schliemann (the Gennadius library copy, for example, has a presentation inscription from Schliemann). The draft of the manuscript for this book and the diaries on which it is based are in the Gennadius library. The book is exceedingly rare today: I have never seen a copy offered for sale. *La Chine* was reprinted as *Reise durch China und Japan im Jahre 1865* (Konstanz 1984) and in Japanese (not seen by me) as *Nihon Chogoku ryokoki* in *Shin ikoku sosho*, series 2, volume 6, Tokyo 1982. The NUC lists only three copies in the United States.

1869a. *Ithaque le Péloponnèse Troie: Recherches archéologiques*. Paris: c. Reinwald (15, Rue des Saints-Pères). [xvi] + 232 pp. Small 8vo. 20 cm. Four lithographs and 2 maps.

This book was issued in printed paper wrappers, the equivalent of a modern paperback book, with the author's name appearing on the title page as "Henry Schliemann." This is the first of Schliemann's archaeological publications, and as such it should appear at the beginning of any list of Schliemann's writings. It launched his career as an archaeologist and its success fueled his enthusiasm. The title of this work as it appears printed on the title page lacks the conjunction "et" between Péloponnèse and Troie, but it is almost always cited, even by Schliemann himself, as *Ithaque, le Péloponnèse et Troie*.

An extensive description of the Greek journey that formed the basis of this book is given by Traill (1995, 40–58), and here it is sufficient to note that the book describes Schliemann's explorations of the supposed site of Odysseus's palace on the island of Ithaka and gives details of Schliemann's short, and very amateurish, trial excavations there over a period of two days. He also visited sites in the Peloponnese, most importantly the sites of Mycenae and Tiryns, which were the objects of his research much later. But the importance of this book is found in Schliemann's enthusiastic acceptance of Frank Clavert's identification of Hisarlik in Anatolia as the probable site of Homeric Troy and his first expression of interest in excavating the site. Although Schliemann claims to have identified Hisarlik as the site of Homeric Troy independently of Clavert, there is no doubt that he was in fact persuaded to this view by Clavert during his visit to the Troad in 1868 (Allen 1999, 85–109; Traill 1995, 40–58). Schliemann is credited today with renewing the interest in the question of Troy and popularizing the identification of Hisarlik as Troy to a wider scholarly audience, but *Ithaque* makes little contribution to this topic and is chiefly of historical interest.

Ithaque was published in French and is prefaced with the first of Schliemann's many autobiographical essays that were later to provide the basis of the uncritical biographical writings about Schliemann, such as the biographies by Ludwig and Payne. Traill notes that the French text was submitted to the University of Rostock for a doctorate and was the principal reason for the awarding of the degree to Schliemann, even though some of the passages of description concerning Ithaka had been cribbed from an 1854 travel guide (Traill 1995, 64–65). Before we judge Schliemann too harshly, however, it should be noted that most 18th and 19th century travel writers tended to crib from each other in writing up landscape or topographical descriptions. It is nevertheless true that the importance of *Ithaque* is only evident when the book is viewed in the light of Schliemann's later achievements, and although enthusiastically expressed and earnest in tone it is not a well-structured or important book in itself. The book is neither innovative in style nor visually of any particular interest. There are only two maps, one of Ithaka and a slightly larger folding map of the Troad (in the

French edition), and the plates (signed by Muller) are conventional, often reproduced views of the Acropolis of Athens, the lion gate at Mycenae, the Treasury of Agamemnon [sic], and the Acropolis of Tiryns. There are also three ancient inscriptions transcribed in the text. As a travel book it has the look of a work produced in 1829 rather than 1869, and it would have appeared hackneyed or old-fashioned, one suspects, to Parisian literary society. *Ithaque* does not stand up to the test of time and modern readers will not read it for pleasure as they might read Mark Twain's *Innocents Abroad*, which was published in the same year. *Innocents Abroad*, by way of providing an instructive contrast to Schliemann's book, is rollicking good fun. It is a witty, well-illustrated, always entertaining account of Twain's Mediterranean travels with the "pilgrims" on the *S.S. Quaker city*. In comparison with this gem of travel writing, *Ithaque* is a dull and pretentious book lacking in humor, color, and human feeling.

I examined copies of *Ithaque* in the Boston public library and the Gennadius and Blegen libraries in Athens. I believe that very few copies were printed, possibly fewer than 500 each of the French and German editions. I base this estimate on the present-day rarity of the book. It is possible that most copies of this title were simply given away by Schliemann. The NUC lists five copies in the United States.

1869b. *Ithaka, der Peloponnes und Troja. Archäologische Forschungen. Leipzig*: Commissions-Verlag Giesecke und Devrient. [xx] + 213 pp. [the difference in pagination from 1869a is the result of moving the table of contents to the front]. Small 8vo. 20 cm. four lithographs and 2 maps [maps are in French; the lithographs have been given German captions].

After the appearance of this title in the original French, a German edition was brought out at Schliemann's expense and translated by Carl Andress, the librarian at New Strelitz (Lascarides 1977, 68). The title page is signed as "Heinrich Schliemann." it is perhaps significant that Schliemann wrote his first two publications in French and a German edition was thought necessary only as a translation of the original work. One is led to conclude that the first two works may have taken shape in Schliemann's mind as examples of *travel* writing, a well-established genre of genteel literary production. I believe that he may have intended his European readers, particularly in Paris (his permanent residence at the time, apart from the occasional trip to Indianapolis), to regard these two titles as literary works. One suspects that

the resolution to become an archaeologist and to excavate at Troy took shape
as he was composing the text for *Ithaque* in Paris after his Greek trip (Traill
1995, 57–58 is particularly interesting in this regard). This inspiration or
resolution, once taken, may have prompted him to write the autobiographical
introduction in order to "back date" his interest in archaeology and to explain,
as it were, the swing that is so evident to the reader today from travel
narrative to archaeological report.

This book is very rare today. I have a copy, and I examined another in the
Boston public library. The German text was reprinted by Ernst Meyer,
Wissenschaftliche Buchgesellschaft, Darmstadt, in 1963, 1976, and 1984.
The text of the reprints is photomechanically reproduced, and supplied by
Meyer with a foreword and a name and subject index. The NUC lists nine
copies.

1874a. *Trojanische Alterthümer. Bericht über die Ausgrabungen in Troja.
Leipzig:* In commission bei F.A. Brockhaus. [lvii] + 1 + 319 + 5
unnumbered pages with a table of weights and chemical analyses of bronze
artifacts. Small 8vo. 21 cm.

The title page gives the author's name as "Dr. Heinrich Schliemann" and
has an advertisement for the photographic *Atlas* facing the title page on the
verso of the half title. The price is stated to be 18 thalers. It is bound in heavy
brown printed boards with the image of an anthropomorphic terracotta vase
on the front cover. In the interval between the publication of *Ithaque* in 1869
and the present publication, Schliemann was engaged with divorcing his
Russian wife Katerina, marrying his young Greek wife Sophia, becoming an
archaeologist, and excavating at Troy. This is the report on his first three
seasons of excavation at Troy, which began tentatively (and illegally) in 1870
and were carried on properly and at some length in 1871, 1872, and ending in
June 1873. This is the text volume that accompanied the photographic
portfolio listed below and was issued in French and German versions. This
was Schliemann's first major publication on his excavations at Troy and is
particularly significant because it inaugurated Schliemann's long association
with the *Leipzig* publisher Brockhaus, which continued until his death in
1890. Brockhaus would also bring out a posthumous autobiography
(*Selbstbiographie*) and other significant works related to Schliemann's
research, particularly Schuchhardt's account of Schliemann's excavations.
The text volume was reprinted in Munich and Zurich in 1990, but the

photographic atlas exists in only 500 copies and was never reprinted for reasons discussed below. The only illustrations in the present volume are of the anthropomorphic terracotta vase on the title page and one figure in the text that depicts a pot with an accompanying roll-out of an inscription or line of symbols. The copies I examined are in my own collection, the Boston public library, the Boston Athenaeum, and the Gennadius library. This book is uncommonly encountered on the antiquarian book market today, probably because there were only about 500 copies to go with the *Atlas*. Copies are not hard to find in libraries, however, as the popularity of the subject and of the author were on the rise with this publication. The NUC lists holdings in 18 libraries.

1874b. *Atlas Trojanischer Alterthümer. Photographische Abbildun-gen zu dem Bericht über die Ausgrabungen in Troja. Leipzig*: in commission bei F.A. Brockhaus. 218 photographs mounted individually. 57 pp. 4to. 34 cm.

The author signs his name on the title page as "Dr. Heinrich Schliemann." The printed text that accompanies the *Atlas* consists of descriptions of the plates that vary in length from one line to a long paragraph. The work consists of a portfolio containing 218 bromide photographs by Panagos T. Zapheiropoulos of Athens individually mounted on pieces of heavy paper. There are actually 217 numbered plates, but there are 218 sheets in total because the first plate was printed twice, evidently because Schliemann was dissatisfied with one or both of the prints. The plates I examined measured on average ca. 19 by 28 cm but some were smaller and appear to have been severely trimmed. The quality of the prints, as noted by Lascarides (1977), is very poor. They range from a light greenish-brown to nearly black and are uniformly grainy and indistinct. The first 27 plates consist of photographs of drawings of spindle whorls, axes, pots, beads, figurines, molds, and other artifacts arranged on wooden shelves. Plates 28 to 100 are chiefly photographs of inscriptions, sculptures, pots, metals, and other artifacts, evidently not arranged according to any system or order of classification, but instead stacked or distributed, sometimes one on top of the other, on wooden shelves. Still other photographs record the excavations at Hisarlik (106-109, 111-113, 127-129) or drawings and watercolor sketches with views of the site and the excavations (e.g., 110, 116-118, 157-170, 177-186, 211-216). Finally, as the *chef d'ouevre*, a series of photographs document Priam's Treasure (192-210). Photographs of pithoi, skeletons, coins, and yet more pots occur more or less at random throughout the *Atlas*. The most interesting of the photographs are the handful that were taken on the site showing the excavation trenches and the excavations in progress.

Although these photographs are of very poor quality, they nevertheless represent an invaluable record of Schliemann's excavations at Troy. In the German edition the descriptions of the plates were written on the negatives before printing and are in German, although the plates after number 168 depicting Priam's Treasure have captions in French on the plates (but German in the printed list of captions). The portfolio was printed in an edition of 500 copies at Schliemann's expense (Lascarides 1977), with the photographs as loose plates held in a printed card portfolio closed with string ties. The printed card covers have the title and the image of an anthropomorphic terracotta vessel, which Schliemann took to be a representation of Athena, in the center. The chief purpose of the *Atlas* was to illustrate "Priam's Treasure," a metallic hoard discovered by Schliemann at Troy in 1873, a find considered significant enough by Schliemann for him to bring the excavations to an end. After he smuggled "Priam's Treasure" out of the Ottoman Empire and had it safely lodged in his house at Athens, Schliemann used the hoard to support his identification of Hisarlik as the site of Homeric Troy. The photographic atlas was intended to supply the visual evidence that Hisarlik was indeed rich in gold. Lascarides (1977) says that the photographs were produced between June 1873 and January 1874 and that 100,000 prints were made from the original negatives (25,000 were ultimately rejected as too poor in quality and were not published) and pasted down by hand. Not only is the quality of the photographs very poor, but the negatives and prints evidently deteriorated quickly, which prevented the reprint of the *Atlas*. The public interest was such that the entire issue was sold or given away by March 14, 1874 (Lascarides 1977, 69–70).

The *Atlas* is certainly an unusual publication, and the combination of a printed excavation report with such a large number of original photographic images to accompany the text was an unprecedented innovation. Indeed, Lascarides (1977, 70) claims that this is the first archaeological work to be illustrated with actual photographic prints (as opposed to lithographs made from photographs). The *Atlas* is very rare today. I examined copies of the German edition in the Boston public library and the Gennadius library (James Ferguson's copy, with an original drawing of a spindle whorl laid in, possibly by Schliemann). The NUC lists five holdings, but it does not differentiate between the French and German versions.

1874c. *Atlas des antiquités Troyennes. Illustrations photographiques faisant suite au rapport sur les fouilles de Troie.* Traduit de l'allemand par Alexandre Rizos Rangabé. Paris: Maisonneuve. 218 photographic plates with an explanatory text. [lviii]. 4to. 34 cm.

This is the French version of the *Atlas* with the translated explanatory text to accompany the plates. It was translated from the German by Alexander Rizos Rangabé. This *Atlas* is otherwise identical with the German version and presumably forms part of the original issue of 500 copies, although this is nowhere clearly stipulated. I examined a copy of the French version of the *Atlas* in the Boston Athenaeum. It was printed and distributed by Brockhaus in *Leipzig*, despite the Paris attribution on the title page, and the French publisher handled the distribution in that country.

1874d. *Antiquités Troyennes. Rapport sur les fouilles de Troie.*

Traduit de l'allemand par Alexander Rizos Rangabé. Paris: Maisonneuve and *Leipzig*: F.A. Brockhaus. [lvii],Table des matières [1 leaf], 318 pp + 2 unsigned leaves. 8vo.

This is the French edition of *Trojanische Alterthümer*, translated by Alexander Rizos Rangabé. It appeared shortly after the original German edition was released in *Leipzig*. It was issued, however, without the photographic atlas, evidently because the *Atlas* copies had all been sold or given away before the French edition was published, and the negatives and remaining prints had deteriorated and could not be used to produce more copies of the *Atlas* (Lascarides 1977). The copy I examined in the Gennadius library had printed brown wrappers. The French and German editions of this title in the Gennadius have slightly different collations, and the French edition ends with an additional paragraph dated "Athènes, 1er janvier 1874." The NUC lists five holdings for this title.

1875a. *Troia und seine Ruinen. Vortrag von Dr. Heinrich Schliemann gehalten in der Aula der Universität Rostock den 17. August 1875.* Waren: c. Quandt. 21 pp. Small 4to. 25.5 cm.

This short, unillustrated work is the text of a lecture by Schliemann at the University of Rostock (where he received his doctorate). It is based on his publication of *Trojanische Alterthümer* of the same year. I examined a facsimile copy of the reprint of this title, which appeared with a "Nachbemerkung" and seven illustrations by Konrad Zimmermann (1990, Rostock: Ostsee-Druck Wismar), and I wish to thank professor George Korres for providing me with a copy of this reprint. I also examined a copy of the original in the Gennadius library.

This abstract of his work at Hisarlik is largely taken up with a description of the site and a review of the arguments for regarding it as the site of Homer's Troy (pp. 1–12). Several pages summarize his excavations and describe the finds from the site (pp. 13–15), with particular attention to Priam's Treasure. The lecture concludes with an effort to link the site and the finds from the excavations with Homer's description of Troy. All this can be found in *Troy and its Remains* and the later *Ilios*, and the usefulness of this pamphlet is in Schliemann's efforts to convince the academic community that he had found Troy. It is an exercise in "public relations" made interesting by being related in the first person and thus preserving the "flavor," as it were, of the original lecture. The NUC lists seven holdings for this title.

1875b. *Troy and its Remains: A Narrative of Researches and Discoveries Made on the Site of ilium, and in the Trojan plain.* Edited by Philip Smith, B.A., and translated by Miss l. Dora Schmitz. London: John Murray. With map, plans, views, and cuts. [lv] + 392 pp. 300 illustrations, 2 plans, and 1 map. 8vo. 24 cm. Brown pictorial cloth gilt.

This is the English translation of *Trojanische Alterthümer* with additional information and notes. There is also a helpful concordance of the woodcut illustrations in this book and the photographs in the *Atlas* described above. The book was edited and the concordance compiled by Schliemann's English editor, Philip Smith. Woodcuts were used to illustrate this book because the photographs in the *Atlas* were both poor in quality and in any case unavailable. The elaborate binding has gilt titles on the spine with panels of swastikas at the top and bottom and two designs, a pot and a rosette jewel, as ornaments below the title. The front cover has an elaborate blind stamped floral border with swastikas, four blind rosettes in the corners, and the famous Helios metope from Troy in gilt in the center. The rear cover has the same blind stamped border as the front cover.

The German and French translations of Schliemann's earlier works, published at Schliemann's expense, were issued in relatively small numbers.

John Murray of London purchased the rights for the English translation from Brockhaus for this title, and a large printing was brought out the year following Schliemann's *Leipzig* publication. The larger sales that were anticipated for the English edition contributed to the decision to use numerous woodcuts, a typical choice for illustrated books in this period. It contributed considerably to the publicity connected with Schliemann's excavations and discoveries and their successful reception, and not a little to his fame (Lascarides 1977). This was Schliemann's first taste of the new style of Victorian book production, and the success of this book set the style and standard for all his future publications.

As with all of his later English publications, the title page bears the Americanized form of Schliemann's name, "Dr. Henry Schliemann," which he favored for most of his life (Traill 1995). Underneath his name we are informed that he is a "citizen of the United States of America." one suspects that this peculiar affectation was part of his elaborate plan to divorce his Russian wife, Katerina, for which it was necessary to establish the fact that he was a permanent resident of Indianapolis in order to obtain the divorce (Lilly 1961). It is clear that he was living in Paris when he undertook his first Greek trip (*vide Ithaque*), and by the time that this book was published he had remarried and was living permanently in Athens. Because his Russian wife contested the divorce, it was probably useful to make a public declaration that he was an American citizen. *Troy and its Remains* is usually bound in brown publisher's cloth with the Helios metope, which was a bone of contention between Schliemann and Clavert (Allen 1999, 150–9), illustrated on the front cover. The sculpture was also reproduced in full scale for Schliemann's home in Athens. *Troy and its Remains* contains an autobiographical note by Schliemann dated 1868, presumably a translated version of the introduction from *Ithaque*. A version of this work may be the basis for an Italian edition, *la scoperta di Troia* (Turin, 1962, *vide* de la Fuente 1973), but I have not seen that book.

My description of this title is based on an examination of my own copy. The number of copies published is unknown, but the English edition is likely to have been larger than the German edition, perhaps 1,000 or 1,500 copies. The English edition is found in the antiquarian book trade with some regularity and is much easier to obtain than any of the preceding titles. The NUC lists 22 holdings.

1875c. Συνοπτικὴ ἀφήγησις τῆς γενομένης ἀνακαλύψεως τοῦ Ὁμηρικοῦ Ἰλίου κατὰ τὰ ἔτη 1870, 1871, 1872 καὶ 1873.
Ἀθήνα: Ἀδελφοὶ Πέρρη. 28 pp. One plate and 1 map. 8vo.

Schliemann's own copy of this Greek synopsis of his excavations at Troy is in the Blegen library at the American School of classical Studies at Athens. It is the printed text of an address read before the philological Society "Parnassos" in Athens in February 1875. There is also a copy in the Gennadius library. Both copies have a plate of spindle whorls and a map of the Troad. This work may have been written in Greek by Schliemann as there is no acknowledgement of a translator. It is not in the NUC.

1875. "The Site of the Homeric Troy. Communicated to the Society of Antiquaries, read June 24th, 1875 by Dr. Henry Schliemann."
Archaeologia XLIV: 1-24.

This is the text of Schliemann's lecture before the Society of Antiquaries at Burlington House in London, which was attended by many dignitaries, including William Gladstone. This presentation was well received, and is the subject of an oft-reprinted woodcut illustration depicting Schliemann addressing a packed audience with Gladstone prominently depicted in the center. This lecture was instrumental in assuring a positive reception of Schliemann's theories in Great Britain. It is illustrated with a map of the Troad, plates of pottery, two plates depicting Priam's Treasure, and one plate of a stone mold. *Archaeologia* is a journal available in most scholarly libraries.

1876. *Troy and its Remains: A Narrative of Researches and Discoveries Made on the Site of ilium, and in the Trojan Plain.*
New York: Scribner, Welford and Armstrong. [lv] + 393 pp. 300 illustrations, 51 plates, and 2 maps.

This is the American edition of *Troy and Its Remains*. I have been unable to examine a copy of this edition and the bibliographic information was obtained from Korres. There are reprints by Benjamin Blom, New York, 1968 and Arno, New York, 1976 widely available today. The NUC lists seven holdings for this title.

1878a. *Mycenae: A Narrative of Researches and Discoveries at Mycenae and Tiryns*. Preface by the Right Honorable W.E. Gladstone, M.P. edited by Philip Smith. London: John Murray. [lxviii] + 384 pp. 549 illustrations showing more than 700 objects and 21 plates, 4 colored plates, and 8 plans. Large 8vo. 23.5 cm. Pictorial cloth gilt, invariably has "Mycenae & Tiryns" on the spine.

Schliemann began his excavations at Mycenae in 1876, and his discovery of the Shaft graves in August of that year was perhaps one of his two greatest archaeological achievements. The English format is smaller than the American version published in the same year in New York. It is a medium octavo and about the same size as *Troy and its Remains*, the first book of Schliemann's published by Murray. My copy is bound in a maroon red publisher's cloth with gilt titles on the spine and bands of gilt decoration at the top and bottom. The bull's head rhyton from Shaft grave IV is stamped in blind on the spine except for its gilded horns. The front cover has a border of guilloche and spirals (in black) with four ornaments in the corners based on gold disks also from Shaft grave IV. The central panel of the front cover depicts the lion gate in gold with the heads of the lions restored and the title "Mycenae" in blind on the lintel block and Schliemann's name, gilt, in the doorway above the figure of Greek workman holding a spade. Advertisements for Murray's publications are bound at the end.

Mycenae begins with a description of Schliemann's trial excavations at Tiryns (which seems like something of an afterthought in this book, perhaps reflected also in the full title), and then turns to a detailed description of the topography of Mycenae. The book then settles down to a sober and detailed assessment of the site of Mycenae and sets out the results of the excavations with a level of clarity and assurance that clearly reveals Schliemann's growing mastery of archaeological field methods and the medium of the written word. The many learned disquisitions, backed with a substantial critical apparatus of citations and quotations of original texts, were calculated to persuade scholars to accept his discoveries and attributions. At the same time, the many colorful passages that describe his discoveries in thrilling terms were aimed at the general reader. The illustrations, especially the large folding plates showing views of the site and the Shaft grave circle (with Sophia, Heinrich, and visiting dignitaries amidst their workmen) contributed to the appeal of the book and the enjoyment of the reader. The brightly colored plates of artifacts are an appealing part of the book and a feature of scholarly publications then and now available only to wealthy authors like Schliemann who could subsidize the cost of production and printing. Many passages, such as the description of the visit of the emperor of brazil to the excavations and the dinner for him given by Schliemann in the Treasury of Atreus, the enormous, and splendidly-preserved, tholos tomb at Mycenae, served the double purpose of entertaining general readers and contributing to Schliemann's self-image as an important figure performing on an international stage.

The running heads give the present-day reader some feeling for the excitement and enthusiasm that shines forth from every page. Taking chapter Viii as an example (reporting on the fourth shaft grave), the running heads tell the story: They begin simply with "an altar upon a tomb," "copper vessels: no soldering," "wonderful cow-head," "heap of swords and lances," "golden portrait masks," "archaic seal-rings," and a "battle scene on a ring." These entertaining legends reflect Schliemann's own building excitement as they continue with "massive golden bracelet," "splendid golden crown," "gold soldered with borax," "curious golden goblets," "wonderful *depas amphikypellon*," "the Nestorian goblet," and a "splendidly ornamented cup." As the running heads continue, one can almost feel a sense of building enthusiasm: "objects of Egyptian porcelain," "curious golden diadems," "ornamented gold ribbon, etc.," "symbol of the double axe," "stag of silver and lead," "wonderful cross-buttons," "curious gold buttons," "magnificent gold buttons [these ornaments are illustrated on the front cover of the book]," "gold model of a temple," "gold sword-handle knobs," "Homeric tripods," "Mycenean [sic] swords like rapiers," and finally, a "golden dragon, with crystal scales." Schliemann uses a sequence of adjectives in these heads, for example "curious," "splendid," "wonderful," and "magnificent," to build to a climax and infuse his finds with his own enthusiasm and thrill of discovery. Admit it: Wouldn't you want to read this book after perusing such a list? It is a spectacular book and was a roaring success.

As the following entries in the handlist make clear, the book appeared in a blizzard of translations and in a variety of issues with different colors of publisher's cloth. No one could overlook or ignore this book, and as much as the discovery of Troy, this book was responsible in my opinion for Schliemann's immediate and lasting international fame.

The English and American editions of *Mycenae* are the most commonly encountered of Schliemann's writings in the market for antiquarian books, which is an indication of the large number of copies put into circulation. The size of the printings is nowhere explicitly stated, but would have been several thousand copies. The English edition of *Mycenae* by John Murray alone was likely to be on the order of 1,500–2,000 copies. (*Ilios*, 1880b, by the same publisher, was issued in an edition of about 1,200 copies.) They regularly appear in antiquarian catalogues and are found in most respectable library collections. The NUC lists 12 holdings for the English edition.

1878b. *Mycenae: A Narrative of Researches and Discoveries at Mycenae and Tiryns.* Preface by the Right Honorable W.E. Gladstone, M.P. New York: Scribner, Armstrong, and company. [lxviii] + 384 pp. 549, illustrations and maps, 8 plans, 7 plates in text, 4 colored plates of terracotta figurines, and 14 monotype plates at the end. 4to. 26 cm. Blue or red pictorial cloth gilt, invariably with "Mycenae & Tiryns" on the spine.

The American edition of this book was released at the same time, December 1878, as the edition published by John Murray in London. It was published under the name of Dr. Henry Schliemann, as were all of his English-language books. He had learned something by now, not only about archaeological fieldwork and excavation practice, but also about publicity and the proper forms of publication that were effective in presenting his discoveries to a mixed audience of professional scholars and general readers. *Troy and its Remains* had been Schliemann's largest book up to this point at a respectable 24 by 15 cm and 392 pages with about 500 illustrations. *Mycenae*, however, weighed in at the substantially larger trim size of 26 by 19 cm (the size of a small quarto volume) with nearly 700 images (the number of pages, however, was about the same).

The binding is elaborately decorated publisher's cloth, with fine gilt images, most famously showing Sophia Schliemann standing before the entrance of the tholos tomb she excavated. It is a big, thick, square book with real heft and gravitas. Perhaps not coincidently, Schliemann leaves out his signature autobiographical preface, and its place is taken by an essay from the pen of William Gladstone, the former prime Minister of England.

This book is thus different in many ways from Schliemann's earlier publications, and his text reflects the new maturity of his archaeological work and his growing self-confidence (as opposed to the mere bluster and self-congratulation that one finds *Inthaque* (1869a) or *Troy and Its Remains* (1875b). The publisher's cloth has elaborate pictorial decoration, which differs from the English edition and is found in two states: blue and red. The American editions have gilt titles on the spine, with patterned panels at top and bottom of the spine. The bull's head rhyton (the "wonderful cow-head" of chapter Viii) from the Shaft graves is stamped on the spine in gold and silver. The front cover has two bands of ornaments at the top and bottom with elaborate gold ornaments from the Shaft graves, which appear to be suspended from the bands. A gold belt or headband is draped in *trompe l'oeil*, over the top band. The central panel is ornamented with a view of the Tomb of Clytemnestra with Sophia Schliemann standing by the entrance (taken from a photograph), blind stamped and highlighted with gold. The title, *Mycenae*, is printed in black, and "Schliemann," is in gold. The number printed for any edition is unknown but is likely to be on the order of two or three thousand copies per edition. The American edition is common today and is certainly the easiest of the titles to find in the antiquarian book market. The NUC lists 23 holdings for this book, a reflection of its popularity in the United States.

1878c. *Mykenae: Bericht über meine Forschungen und Entdeckungen in Mykenae und Tiryns. Leipzig*: F.A. Brockhaus. [lxvi] + 447 pp. 549 illustrations, 7 lithographs, 4 colored plates, and 21 other plates. 8vo.

The German text of this book was written by Schliemann at the same time as the English original and was published simultaneously with the London edition. The *Leipzig* edition was produced in a smaller format, an average-sized octavo similar in size to the *Tiryns* edition. This text was reprinted photomechanically by Ernst Meyer, Wissenschaftliche Buchgesellschaft, Darmstadt, in 1964 and 1973 and is provided with a foreword and a list of recent literature supplied by Meyer and dated 1963. I examined a copy of the original in the Blegen library in Athens. The NUC lists four holdings.

1879. *Mycènes: Récit des recherches et découvertes faites à Mycènes et à Tirynthe.* Avec une Préface de M. Gladstone. Translated from English by Professor J. Girardin. Paris: M.M. Hachette. [6] + 488 pp. 549 illustrations, 9 plans, and 7 lithographs. 4to.

This is the French edition of this title, published the year following the publication of the English, German, and American editions. The color plates in the UK and US editions are here found in black and white woodcuts. The binding on the French edition is the most beautiful and finely crafted binding on any of Schliemann's books. It is a deep red pictorial publisher's cloth with a pebbly texture. The lion gate is stamped in gold on the front cover and is highlighted in red and black to create a dazzling chiaroscuro effect. A jumble of rocks and bare-branched bushes block the gate in wild profusion, and the title *Mycènes* is in the opening of the gateway in rustic letters. There is a black border with rows of running spirals and long-necked birds in red. The corners have gilt ornaments reproducing the gold disks from the Shaft graves, with pendent gilt octopi at the top. The same images, a bit simplified, are stamped in black on the back cover, without the decorations in the borders, creating an effect something like the ghostly negative of a photograph. The entire effect is romantic, sensuous, and splendid.

My description is based on my own copy. Copies are found also in the Gennadius and Blegen libraries in Athens. The NUC lists only two holdings.

1880a. Mycenae: A Narrative of Researches and Discoveries at Mycenae and Tiryns. A New edition with important additions and new plates. New York: Scribner, Armstrong, and company. [lxviii] + 404 pp. More than 700 illustrations, maps, 8 plans, 7 plates in text, 4 colored plates of terracotta figurines, and 14 monotype plates at end. 4to. 24 cm.

This title was the most successful of Schliemann's publications, and less than two years after publication a new edition was called for in America, with 16 pages of new text, four new appendices, and two new plates. The trim size of this volume is 2 cm smaller than the first addition. The "important" additions are not indicated in the table of contents, but the text illustrations appear to have increased from about 550 to 700 in number.

The description of this title is based on my own copy. This edition has been reprinted many times, for example, by Benjamin Blom, New York, 1967; by Arno, New York, 1976; and most recently by Ayer, Salem, New Hampshire, in 1989. The NUC lists 19 holdings.

1880b. Ilios: The city and country of the Trojans: The Results of Researches and Discoveries on the Site of Troy and Throughout the Troad in the years 1871–72–73–78–79. Includes an autobiography of the author. London: John Murray. [xvi] + 800 pp. 1,570 illustrations, 1 map, 6 lithographs, and 30 plates. Large 8vo. 25 cm. Pictorial blue or gold cloth gilt.

The copies I examined were bound in blue or gold cloth with gilt titles on the spine and panels of rosettes at the top and bottom. A border of rosettes and gilt figures of Greek and Scythian warriors is found in panels on the front cover. Here, as is usual now, Schliemann signed the cover as "Dr. Henry Schliemann," the name blocked in gold in a separate panel.

This book was written to present the results of the new excavations that Schliemann undertook at Troy in 1878 and 1879. He used the occasion to review the research at Troy from their beginning in 1871, no doubt intending this book to be his final comprehensive publication of the campaigns at Troy. To the eyes of the professional archaeologist, this book looks like a proper site report. After yet another autobiographical introduction, Schliemann gets down to work with this book, with contributions by no less than 11 specialists, some of whom (Mahaffy, Müller, Sayce, and Virchow) were among the leading European scientists and scholars of the day. Their contributions range from a description of the botany of the Troad and an analysis of the copper objects from the excavations to Müller's contribution on the symbolism and meaning of the swastikas found on spindle whorls and other terracotta artifacts.

This is the most extensively illustrated of Schliemann's books, with a total of 1,800 images. Gone, however, are the fine colored plates and the artistic folding panoramas of Mycenae, which are replaced with workman-like maps, plans, and folding plates that show detailed sections from the trenches to illustrate the stratification of the site. At the end of the book are numerous plates of the many spindle whorls bearing scratched symbols and designs. All of the illustrations are woodcuts of a decidedly plain appearance, much less interesting than the fine illustrations found in *Troy and Its Remains* and *Mycenae*.

The overall physical appearance of this volume is that of a "scientific" work rather than a book of adventure and discovery. It is a report that attempts to document the site in its context and to offer a record of the many artifacts discovered in the course of the excavations in a form that would be recognized by a professional readership. Gone also are the sensational running heads: here they are no more exciting than "owl-headed vases," "various tripod-vases," "awls of bone and horn," "another gold diadem," and "pottery of the fourth city" (note the lack of superlative adjectives). There are no colorful anecdotes involving dramatic discoveries, telegrams to the King of the Hellenes, or the entertainment of emperors, which made *Mycenae* a lively and successful book.

A telling detail for the modern archaeologist is the string of nine appendices at the back of the book by the specialists. These appendices are not particularly important or relevant to the main body of the text and are printed in small type in double columns to save space and cut costs. These are features found today, for better or for worse, in most excavation reports. *Ilios*, therefore, is an interesting book, but not a particularly entertaining one. Schliemann is here attempting to establish once and for all that his archaeological discoveries at Troy were of lasting importance and would have to be taken seriously by scholars at the time of publication and in the future. A measure of how seriously Schliemann wished this book to be taken can be seen in the size of the index: *Ilios* has 49 pages, while *Troy and its Remains* has fewer than 11 pages and *Mycenae* fewer than 8 pages of index.

According to Traill (1995, 196–209), *Ilios* was published simultaneously in the German, English, and American editions on 10 November 1880, but some copies have the date of 1881 (see below). Murray apparently produced an edition of about 1,200 copies and it is likely that the other editions were printed in similar numbers. Certainly copies are readily found today, although less common than either *Mycenae* or *Tiryns*, on the antiquarian book market. The NUC lists nine holdings.

1880c. *Ilios: The city and country of the Trojans: The Results of Researches and Discoveries on the Site of Troy and Throughout the Troad in the years 1871–72–73–78–79. Including an autobiography of the author.* New York: Harper and brothers. [xvi] + 800 pp. Woodcuts in the text illustrating about 1,800 artifacts [an exact count is not given and collation is difficult as the numbering sequence of artifacts is not continuous], 1 map, 6 plans, and 32 lithographic plates of engraved spindle whorls bound at the end [which are included in the count of artifact illustrations on the title page]. Large 8vo. 25 cm. Red pictorial cloth gilt.

The American edition of this title has the date of 1880 on the copyright page. Korres gives the date as 1881 (with 1880 in parentheses). The NUC rather confusingly lists copies under both dates. My personal copy, once owned by Carl Blegen, has the date of 1881, but I have a copy with no date at all. Presumably the book was copyrighted and the printing was done in New York beginning in November or December 1880 as the printed sheets used for typesetting arrived from London, but the book was not released until early 1881, and there may be more than one issue or state of this edition. The author's name appears on the title page as "Dr. Henry Schliemann." This volume is slightly smaller than the other publications from New York, *viz.* *Tiryns* and *Mycenae*, which are large and square enough to be classed as small quartos. This edition is a large octavo. *Ilios* was reprinted by Benjamin Blom, New York, 1968, and the original is commonly available on the antiquarian book market, where it is indeed one of the three, with *Mycenae* and *Tiryns*, most often offered. The NUC lists five holdings for 1880 and 22 holdings for 1881.

1880d. Heinrich Schliemann, ed., James Ferguson, *Das Erechtheion und der Tempel der Athene Polias in Athen. Leipzig*: F.A. Brockhaus. Translated from English by Dr. Ludwig Meyer. [2] + 30 pp. Two woodcut illustrations and 4 plates. 4to. Three paragraph introduction by Dr. Heinrich Schliemann date September 1879 in London.

This is one of Schliemann's few contributions to the publication of another scholar. James Ferguson was an English artist and architect and an early supporter of Schliemann. Schliemann wrote the introduction for this translation of Ferguson's study of the Erechtheion, which was originally published in London in 1876. He contributed financially to having it published Byrockhaus. It is one of Schliemann's rare forays into classical archaeology. Despite his clear interest exhibited by many visits to classical sites in Greece and Italy and his enthusiasm for the classical languages he seemed to have little interest in excavations or sustained research in that field. I examined the copy in the Gennadius library.

1881a. *Ilios: Stadt und land der Trojaner: Forschungen und Entdeckungen in der Troas und besonders auf der Baustelle von Troja. Leipzig*: F.A. Brockhaus. [xxiv] + 880 pp. 1,570 text illustrations, 8 folding plans, 1 map, and 32 plates. Large 8vo.

According to Traill (1995, 196–209) this edition was published 10 November 1880 although it bears the imprint 1881. It was translated into German from Schliemann's English by three translators hired by Brockhaus in *Leipzig*. I have not examined a copy. The NUC lists six holdings for this title.

1881b. *Reise in der Troas im Mai 1881. Leipzig*: F.A. Brockhaus.

(2) + 77. One map. 8vo.

The purpose of this publication was to contribute to the topographical study of the Troad and northwestern Turkey, and it appears to have been carried out in part to answer those critics who continued to cast doubt on Hisarlik as the site of Homeric Troy. Schliemann realized that a detailed survey and accurate map were necessary to counter these critics, and his own personal familiarity with the other sites in the region, both classical and prehistoric, was not complete enough to convince his critics that no other site comparable to Hisarlik was to be found in the Troad. This survey was necessary to supplement Schliemann's firsthand knowledge of local topography. It was the last of the classic topographic investigations to be carried out in the 18th and 19th centuries, and comparable explorations would not be undertaken until the 1930s in connection with the University of Cincinnati explorations of Troy and in the 1990s with the surveys conducted by members of the University of Tübingen excavation team at Troy.

I examined my own copy, which as light blue printed wrappers, and copies in the Gennadius and Blegen libraries in Athens. An English translation of this text was published as an appendix to the English edition of *Troja* (John Murray, London, 1884) with the title, "Journey in the Troad." The NUC lists only three holdings for *Reise*.

1881c. Orchomenos: Bericht über meine Ausgrabungen im Böotischen Orchomenos. Leipzig: F.A. Brockhaus. [vi] + 58 pp. Nine illustrations and 4 plates.

The German text appears to be the only edition to be published in book form except for the Greek translation released in Athens. The German book was translated by Schliemann himself from the English text that was published in the *Journal of Hellenic Studies* the same year (Traill 1995, 213; see below). The failure to bring out French, English, and American editions of this book is unusual for Schliemann, and we can only surmise that he was either uninterested in pursuing his research at Orchomenos or was distracted by his need to renew excavations at Troy. I examined my personal copy of this book, which has gray printed wrappers, and a copy in the Gennadius library. It is a rare book. Copies of this title appear only rarely on the antiquarian book market. The NUC lists eight holdings for this title.

1881d. "Exploration of the Boeotian Orchomenus." Journal of Hellenic

Studies 2:122–63. One map, 1 plan, 12 woodcuts, and 2 plates.

The article is illustrated with a map of the site, four woodcuts showing architectural elements from the tholos tomb, a plan of the tomb, eight woodcuts illustrating sherds, (evidently Middle Helladic Minyan ware), three or four inscriptions, and two plates of the roof of the side chamber of the tholos made from drawings by Dörpfeld and his colleagues. The article, which was translated for the German edition of *Orchomenos*, is the English language report on Schliemann's excavations at Orchomenos. This text was also brought out in a Greek translation by Sophia Schliemann and published in Athens. At this point in Schliemann's career his publishers, or at least John Murray of London, were concerned about the poor sale of the large and heavily illustrated excavation reports on Mycenae and Troy. Murray, for instance, had to be persuaded by James Ferguson to risk the costs of the publication of the Tiryns excavations (Traill 1995, 239). Schliemann himself evidently did not have sufficient interest in Orchomenos to push for further translations and he appears to have been content with this form of publication. This is not the only case where his excavations were published in cursory form. His excavations at Marathon were published in the article cited below and his various travels and trial excavations in Italy, Kythera, and the Peloponnese were never fully published at all or appeared only in short articles in newspapers and periodical magazines (e.g., Korres 1974, 28, items 204–6 on his excavations at Thermopylae and 34–5, items 240–1 on his exploration of Kythera).

The article begins with a lengthy description of the journey from Athens to Orchomenos with much topographical detail. Schliemann then describes the sites, with a thorough review of the ancient texts and modern traveler's accounts that mention the site. He describes his excavations of the collapsed tholos tomb, which he calls "the treasury." Finally, he describes his excavations in the town. He was unable to date, at this point in his career, the earlier prehistoric levels at the site (Neolithic to early bronze Age), but he had a keen eye for detail and his ability to discriminate between the Mycenaean pottery on the site and the unknown, and undated, glazed pottery of the Neolithic period was innovative, considering that he did not know what he was looking at. The *Journal of Hellenic Studies* is commonly available in scholarly libraries.

1882a. *Catalogue des Trésors de Mycènes au Musée d'Athènes avec un plan de l'acropole de Mycènes dans lequel toutes mes fouilles sont bien indiquées. Leipzig*: F.A. Brockhaus. (2) + 57 pp. One map. 16mo (i.e., smaller than a 12mo). ca. 17 cm (estimated).

The text was intended to accompany the Schliemann rooms with the exhibition of the finds from the Mycenaean excavations in the polytechnic University in Athens. Today these materials are exhibited in newly renovated rooms facing the entrance of the National Museum in Athens. I examined a copy of this fragile ephemeron in the Gennadius library. The NUC has six holdings for this title.

1882b. *Περιήγησις ἀνὰ τὶν Τρῳάδα κατα Μάϊον τοῦ 1881*. Ἀθήνα: Παρνασσοῦ. Translated from German by P.G. Kastromenos. 50 pp. 8vo. 24 cm.

This is a Greek translation by Schliemann's brother-in-law of the 1881 publication of *Reise in der Troas*. The copy in the Gennadius library has pink printed wrappers. Schliemann's own copy, with a dedication in Greek by the translator, is in the Blegen library of the American School of classical Studies at Athens. The NUC lists locate only one copy in the University of Cincinnati library.

1883. *Ὀρχομενός. Ὑπόμνημα ἐπι τῶν ἐν τῷ Βοιωτικῷ Ὀρχομενῷ ἀνασκαφῶν αὐτοῦ*. Ἀθήνα: Ἀνδρέου Κορομυλᾶ. Translated from German by Sophia Schliemann. [ii] + 60 pp. Nine illustrations and 4 plates. 8vo. 23 cm.

This is the Greek edition of *Orchomenos* (1881), translated from German by Sophia Schliemann. A copy inscribed by Sophia Schliemann is in the Gennadius library. It has gray printed wrappers and a title page printed in red and black. It has the same illustrations and plates as the German edition, but with Greek legends. A second copy, also inscribed by Mrs. Schliemann, is in the Blegen library of the American School of classical Studies. The NUC lists one holding in the University of Cincinnati library.

1884a. *Troja: Ergebnisse meiner neuesten Ausgrabungen auf der Baustelle von Troja, in den Heldengräbern, bunarbaschi und andern Orten der Troas im Jahre 1882*. Mit Vorrede von A. H. Sayce. *Leipzig*: F.A. Brockaus. [xlv] + 462 pp. 150 woodcuts and 4 maps and plans in lithography. 8vo. 24 cm.

This is the German edition of the UK edition of *Troja* (1884b) published by John Murray. The text of *Troja* appeared also in an American edition. The copy I examined is in the Blegen library of the American School at Athens. The book was reprinted by Rainer Gerlach, Harenberg, Dortmund, 1984 (2nd issue 1987). The NUC lists one copy in the Yale University library.

1884b. *Troja: Results of the latest Researches and Discoveries on the Site of Homer's Troy, and in the Heroic Tumuli and other Sites, Made in the Year 1882; and a Narrative of a Journey in the Troad in 1881*. London: John Murray. [xl] + 434 pp. illustrated with 150 woodcuts, 4 maps, and plans. Large 8vo. 24 cm.

The London edition is bound in green pictorial cloth. The spine has gilt titles at top and bottom and is decorated with an elaborate image of a distaff and a spindle whorl with engraved swastikas on it, connected by a long thread of yarn, all in gold. The front cover has the image of an owl on a floral arabesque above the title, which is an even more elaborate acanthus arabesque, that to my eyes looks like a giant S enclosing the figure of a woman in Classical dress (Helen?) holding a distaff and spindle. This was the last book on Troy written by Schliemann in his lifetime.

Troja opens with a long preface by A.H. Sayce of oxford who comments at length on the Homeric question. Schliemann's text follows without the usual autobiographical introduction, summarizing Schliemann's travel in the Troad and excavation at Troy in 1881 and 1882. This is a businesslike volume published as an octavo without the folding plans and color plates that adorn his other works. Except for a map of the Troad and two plans of Troy, there are no large plates. The volume is a measured treatise focusing on the analysis of the results of 10 years study at Troy, which is examined systematically layer by layer, settlement by settlement, from the bottom up. The seven successive cities at Troy, as they were recognized in 1882, are covered in the first five chapters. A sixth chapter describes the burial tumuli in the Troad and a seventh chapter discusses the other archaeological sites in the Troad. At the end of the text there are no less than 17 separate notes (as they are called), which cover everything from ancient authors and topographers, to cults, chickens, spindle whorls, and the use of precious metals as money. Further adding to the heft and scholarly gravitas of the book are seven lengthy appendices that include the English translation of Schliemann's account of his journey in the Troad, a dissertation on human bones by Virchow, and meteorological observations at Hisarlik by Schliemann himself. According to Traill (1995, 239), Murray found the sales of *Ilios* and *Troja* disappointing after the success of *Mycenae*, no doubt because of Schliemann's decision to make his publications more "scientific," rather than writing for the general public.

I examined my own copy. A copy in the Blegen library of the American School has a long inscription in Greek by Schliemann, dedicating the book to Eugene Schuyler, the American minister in Athens. This title is readily available today on the antiquarian market. The NUC lists four copies of this title.

1884c. *Troja: Results of the latest Researches and Discoveries on the Site of Homer's Troy and in the Heroic Tumuli and other Sites, Made in the Year 1882; and a Narrative of a Journey in the Troad in 1881.* New York: Scribners. (40) + 434 pp. 150 woodcuts, 4 maps, and plans. 8vo. 24 cm.

The American edition of the title was published by John Murray in London (1884b). I examined my own copy of this work, and it is identical to the London edition. It is certainly more common: The NUC lists 33 holdings of this title in US libraries. The text was reprinted by Benjamin Blom, New York, 1967.

1884d. "Das sogenannte Grab der 192 Athener in Marathon." *Zeitschrift für ethnologie. Organ der Berliner Gesellschaft für Anthropologie, ethnologie und Urgeschichte.* Berlin: A. Asher, pp. 85–88.

In this short article Schliemann relates how he became suspicious of the attribution of a tumulus in the Marathon plain as being that of the Athenians who fell in the 5th century battle of Marathon. He noted the large number of obsidian blades and projectile points to be found on the tumulus and surmised that these indicated an age for the tumulus far older than the traditional fifth century. He compared the tumulus to similar ones he investigated in the Troad, and his subsequent short test excavation of the Marathon tumulus convinced him that it was indeed a prehistoric tumulus. These excavations were never fully published and this is the only printed record of the excavation. The mound is today considered as the burial mound of the Athenians who fell at Marathon, following the discovery of the burials (which were found below the level investigated by Schliemann). He appears to have been frustrated by the high water level in the plain and did not dig deeply enough to find the burials himself.

1885a. *Tiryns: The prehistoric palace of the Kings of Tiryns: The Results of the latest excavations*. Preface by professor f. Adler, and contributions by Dr. Wm. Dörpfeld. New York: Charles Scribner's Sons. [lxiv] + 385 pp. 189 woodcuts, 24 plates in chromolithography, 1 map, 4 plans. Large 8vo. 26 cm. Red pictorial cloth gilt, identical with the London edition.

This is the American edition of this title. Although this book is large, thick, and square, and has been described as a quarto, the collation shows it is in fact a large octavo. With this book, Schliemann returned to the grand style of Victorian publishing. The publisher's cloth binding on the English and American editions are found in a deep brick red and a royal blue. The colored plates in this book, which were used to create the sumptuous decorations for the cover and the spine, are reproductions of paintings made by Emile Gilliéron. The British and American editions of *Tiryns* are the same trim size as the 1878 editions of *Mycenae*, but the bindings are the most decorative and elaborate of all of Schliemann's publications. The spine has gilt titles, an ornament, and bands of running spirals, while an elaborate border of running spirals and small squares frames the front cover. Four stylized palmettes fill the corners and draw the eye to the large bull-leaper device and titles in the central panel. The exclusive use of gold for all the ornaments and titles on the bright blue or maroon red publisher's cloth creates a splendid sight. The top edge of the text block of the copy I examined was also gilt. When found in good condition, the bindings used for *Tiryns* are very impressive examples of Victorian book arts. The effect of luxury and the sumptuous use of materials is enhanced by the subtly patterned end papers and the 24 high quality four-color chromolithographs, the most used by Schliemann in any one publication. Several of these plates fold out, and all are strikingly beautiful. Dörpfeld's fine foldout architectural plans are also partly printed in color.

The book is a *tour de force* of printing and publishing. For an assessment of this book's contents and archaeological value, see the annotations to the English edition, *Tiryns* (1886a) below. I examined my own copy of this title, along with numerous copies in libraries and bookshops. This text was reprinted by Benjamin Blom, New York, 1967. The NUC lists 24 copies of this title.

1885b. *Tirynthe: le palais préhistorique des rois de Tirynthe: Résultat des dernières fouilles.* Paris: Reinwald. [lxvi] + 401 pp. One map and 27 plates. Large 8vo. 27.5 cm.

The French edition of this work was published simultaneously with the other editions. I have been unable to determine whether it was translated from the German original or was written, as is likely, by Schliemann himself at the same time as he was writing the German text. My description is based on an examination of my own imperfect copy. The NUC lists only two holdings for this book.

1885c. *Ilios: Ville et pays des Troyens: Résultat des fouilles sur l'emplacement de Troie et des explorations faites en Troade de 1871 à 1882 avec une autobiographie de l'auteur.* Paris: [Librairie Firmin-Didot?] Reinwald. Translated by Mrs. Emile Egger, with three additional appendices. [xii] + 1032. 1721 illustrations, 32 plates, 8 plans, and 2 maps. Large 8vo. 30 cm.

The French translation of *Ilios* was considerably delayed and only appeared five years after the English and German editions. In the interval, Schliemann had published *Troja* (1884b), and a translation of this text was included with this edition of *Ilios* according to Traill (Traill 1995, 249). I examined a copy in the Blegen library of the American School at Athens. It is uncommonly encountered on the antiquarian book market. The NUC lists four copies of this title.

1886a. *Tiryns: The prehistoric palace of the Kings of Tiryns: The Results of the latest excavations. London*: John Murray. [lxiv] + 385 pp. 178 illustrations, 24 chromolitho-graphed plates, 4 plans, and 1 map. Large 8vo. 25.5 cm. Blue pictorial cloth gilt.

This is the London edition of this title. The copy I examined appears to be identical with the American edition, although it is about one-half centimeter shorter in height and appears to be printed on thicker paper stock. It has gilt titles on the spine and on the front cover a border of running spirals with large palmettes in the corners frames a reproduction of the bull leaper painting in the center of the front cover underneath the title. The author's name, "Dr. Henry Schliemann" appears below the bull leaper. The titles and decoration are all gilt. The English edition has the same design as the front cover stamped in blind on the back cover, something not found on the American edition.

The original text was written by Schliemann and Dörpfeld in German and was translated into English by John Mahaffy. According to Traill (1995, 249) the German, French, UK, and US editions were published simultaneously. The different publishers were persuaded to undertake this work on a cost-sharing basis and were influenced by Murray's decision to publish, which in part resulted from the arguments of James Ferguson (Traill 1995, 239–42). This title bears the imprint of 1885, as do the French and American editions, while the English edition has the date of 1886. No doubt this difference is because of the fact that the English edition did not appear until the end of 1885. The book is dedicated to James Ferguson, the author of *Das Erechthion* and a staunch Schliemann supporter. On the title page the author's name is given as "Dr. Henry Schliemann," and he now subjoins an elaborate list of academic titles (all British) including an honorary degree from oxford, a fellowship in the Society of Antiquaries of London, and a membership with a gold medal in the Royal institute of British Architects. No longer content with "citizen of the united States of America" Schliemann emphasizes with this list of academic titles the serious tone and concentrated purpose of this book.

After an extensive introduction to Mycenaean archaeology by Professor Adler, the first chapters cover the excavations, topography, and history of Tiryns, which read like a modern PhD. dissertation in Classics. Then come two long chapters by Schliemann discussing the artifacts recovered in the excavations, and these are followed by two chapters by Wilhelm Dörpfeld, with a description of the architecture and a report on the 1885 excavation season. There is one appendix on imported Baltic amber by Otto Helm.

The tone throughout the work is sober, restrained, descriptive, and scientific. The text is almost entirely free of the usual breathless enthusiasm heretofore exhibited by Schliemann. The opening pages still have the usual personal touches. Schliemann describes his daily routine of rising early, swimming in the bay, having coffee, riding out to the site before dawn, digging until midday, having lunch and a nap before resuming work, followed by a return to the hotel in Nafplion for dinner. He tells us that he and Dörpfeld ate meals of local mutton, fish, vegetables, fruit, tinned corned beef from Chicago, and soup made from meat extract imported from London. He assures the reader that his young assistant Dörpfeld thoroughly enjoyed their shared diet and routine, including their daily naps on the acropolis of Tiryns in the midday sun with rocks for pillows and nothing for shade but their hats over their faces. One wonders. I note that Dörpfeld evidently declined to join Schliemann for his 4 AM routine of swimming in the bay and that he appeared on the site only after daybreak. A sensible fellow, it seems.

The descriptions of the excavations, the site, and the finds that follow are sober, factual, and purely descriptive, with a minimum of purple prose or unsupported speculation. The running heads reflect this sobriety, although they form a narrative of their own. They are shorn of adjectives and superlatives and consist entirely of simple titles: "the name Tiryns," "handled jugs," and "handle in form of an animal" are typical and sufficient to give the reader a flavor of the whole book.

The more restrained tone of this book was not calculated to make it popular with general readers, and one thinks that it was not a bestseller. Clean unmarked copies with no signs of heavy use by readers are commonly available today on the antiquarian book market. To the eye of the practiced bibliophile, this is clear testimony of the failure of this book to attract a large general readership.

When viewed from another perspective, however, this book is Schliemann's best piece of archaeological reporting in the modern mode. Its clear descriptions, cautious evaluation of evidence, attention to detail, and ample illustration of artifacts and features make this book of lasting scientific value and the starting place for the ongoing study of the site of Tiryns and research into the Mycenaean world. It is a fitting way for Schliemann to end his career, at least in terms of writing excavation reports. It shows clearly how well he had mastered the methods of the judicious professional and abandoned the ways of the reckless amateur. I here describe my own copy, and I have examined many other examples in libraries and bookshops. The NUC lists 12 copies.

1886b. *Tiryns: Der prähistorische Palast der Könige von Tiryns: Ergebnisse der neuesten Ausgrabungen.* Mit vorrede von Geh. Oberbaurath prof. F. Adler und beitragen von Dr. W. Dörpfeld. *Leipzig*: F.A. Brockhaus. [lxviii] + 487 pp. 178 illustrations, 24 plates in chromolithography, 1 map, and 4 plans. 4to. 24.5 cm.

Schliemann wrote the text for *Tiryns* in German, as Dörpfeld did for his contributions, and arranged for the German text to be translated into English for the British and American editions. In the copy I examined in the Blegen library of the American School, the front cover has the same gilt decoration as the American and British editions, but the trim size of the book is smaller, an 8vo rather than a 4to, and it is printed on an acidic paper that is now browning and brittle. On the verso of page 487 there is a list of Brockhaus's editions of Schliemann's writings in German. All of the editions of *Tiryns* are commonly encountered in the antiquarian book market. The NUC lists one copy of the German edition in the Yale University library.

> 1891. *Bericht über die Ausgrabungen in Troja im Jahre 1890: Mit einem Vorwort von Sophie Schliemann un Beiträgen von Dr. W. Dörpfeld. Leipzig*: F.A. Brockhaus. 60 pp. One plan, 2 plates, and 4 illustrations. 8vo.

This small book or lengthy pamphlet was issued in printed wrappers. This is the last excavation report to be written in Schliemann's lifetime: He died in Naples in December 1890 and this report was not published until the following year. Sophia Schliemann (although her name in Greek is spelled with a final "a," her publications typically gave her name in the French form "Sophie") and Dörpfeld were able to complete the text and editing. It marks the last word by Schliemann on the question of Homeric Troy. It is very rare. I base my description on my own copy, and a copy in the Gennadius library. Both copies have brown printed wrappers. An edited and abridged translation of this report is found in the UK edition of Schuchhard's *Schliemann's excavations* (1891). The NUC lists six copies of the *Bericht*.

> 1892. *Heinrich Schliemann's Selbstbiographie: Bis zu seinem Tode vervollständigt (von Alfred Brüchner): Herausgegeben von Sophie Schliemann. Leipzig*: F.A. Brockhaus. (5) + 100 pp. One portrait and 10 illustrations. Small 8vo. 22.5 cm.

This posthumously-published book is included in the list of Schliemann's publications because the text was written by Schliemann, although it was compiled after his death by Sophia Schliemann. She supplemented the text with other material at her disposal. The original edition has a useful publisher's catalogue at the end that lists Brockhaus' *Leipzig* publications of Schliemann in German.

I examined my own copy. It is not particularly rare. This title was reprinted by Brockhaus in 1930, 1936, 1939, 1942 (this issue has 136 pages counting preliminary leaves and a pictorial card binding with an image of a two handled cup [depas amphikypellon] on the front cover), 1943, 1944, 1949, 1953, and 1955. These reprints have an afterward (Nachwort) by Ernst Meyer. This text was reprinted again by Ernst Meyer, Wiesbaden, and F.A. Brockhaus in 1961. There are also editions in Italian (*Autobiografia di un archeologo*, Milan 1962), French (*Ma Vie*, translated by Claire Pouzin, Paris 1956), and Hungarian (*Eletem, kalandjaim*, Budapest 1960, according to Korres 1974, 38, item 273). The NUC lists five copies of the first edition.

CONCLUSIONS

The contents of the books catalogued in this handlist should give serious pause to Schliemann's critics. A perusal of the writings of Calder and Traill makes one thing particularly clear: Whatever their contributions to historiography or classical studies, these writers are not practicing field archaeologists. It is not necessary to disagree with the overall negative assessment that they offer of Schliemann's character or of his conduct in business or private life to take a different view of his archaeology. If one places Schliemann's archaeological books on a shelf in their order of publication and reads them through, one is struck by Schliemann's evolving mastery of his subject. It is true that if taken out of this context his early work at Troy leaves much to be desired and deserves the ridicule it often receives today (although I think the accusations of fraud to be unfair; Runnels 1997), but when taken as a whole, his work in later years at Mycenae and Tiryns, and his work at Troy after 1880, displays a professionalism that is hard to deny. For all his faults, Schliemann brought to light the bronze Age Mycenaean civilization, established the archaeological subfield of Aegean prehistory, and popularized archaeology so successfully that his name is still recognized by everyone with an interest in the subject, and to this archaeologist's eyes published some of the best archaeological reports of his or any age.

In my opinion a fruitful new line of scholarly research would be to reexamine Schliemann's career for its contributions to archaeological method and theory. Apart from the short essays of Korres (1990) and Witte (1990), I do not think that this has been properly done. Schliemann was indeed a pioneer in archaeology. To take but one example, Schliemann had a habit of returning to the same site to dig again, almost always driven by criticism to ask new questions and answer old ones with new evidence. In modern terms, he was in the habit of modifying his research design, employing multiple working hypotheses, and modifying his views in the light of new evidence. His entire approach to field archaeology with its attention to method, detail, documentation, typology, comparative study, and publication is worthy of emulation and constitutes a major development in the field. The modern Aegean prehistorian should not shrink from acknowledging his or her indebtedness to Schliemann's innovations, which have been transmitted from generation to generation from Dörpfeld to Blegen down to our own day as a legacy as solid and as useful and at times as colorful as a copy of *Tiryns*.

RELATED WORKS AND REFERENCES

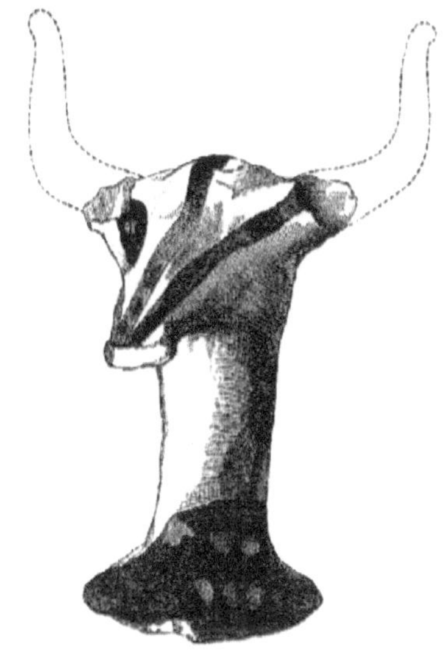

**Idol of Terra-cotta, with a Cow's head, on the handle of a vase.
(Reproduced from H. Schliemann, Mycenae: A Narrative of Researches
and Discoveries at Mycenae and Tiryns [New York 1878] p. 104)**

The following works are listed alphabetically by first author, and not chronologically.

Allen, Susan Heuck. 1999. *Finding the Walls of Troy: Frank Clavert and Heinrich Schliemann at Hisarlik.* Berkeley: University of California Press.

This is the first biography of Frank Clavert, who identified the site of Hisarlik as Homeric Troy. Clavert made a number of other important contributions to the study of prehistoric archaeology (including the first published scientific stratigraphical excavation of a prehistoric site in the Troad). Although Clavert is the central character in this book, Allen includes a great deal of information of relevance to the study of Heinrich Schliemann. Exceptionally well researched and written, this study of Clavert's contributions to the development of prehistoric archaeology is essential reading for anyone wishing to fully appreciate the context of Schliemann's excavations in the Troad. Schliemann had a habit of prefacing his books with autobiographical essays that give the impression that he was a pioneer in this area and worked alone. Although he did not conceal the participation and contributions of people like Clavert, he certainly worked to minimize his indebtedness to them. Schliemann's activities make much more sense when viewed from the perspective of the growth and development of prehistoric archaeology in the 1860s and 1870s and this book is a major contribution to the history of archaeology in this period.

Blegen, Carl W. 1963. *Troy and the Trojans.* New York and Washington: Frederick A. Praeger.

Carl Blegen excavated at Troy in the 1930s for the University of Cincinnati. A brilliant field archaeologist, Blegen's career as an Aegean prehistorian spanned much of the 20th century. This small book, part of the long-lived and very popular *Ancient peoples and places* series edited by the late Glyn Daniel, summarized the results of Blegen's excavations at Troy, and is included here because of its assessment of Schliemann's archaeological abilities. These views must be taken seriously because Blegen was himself one of the masters of fieldwork technique and was in a position to evaluate Schliemann's work at Troy firsthand.

Boetticher, Ernst. 1890. *Hissarlik. Wie es ist.* Berlin.

This pamphlet is an attack on Schliemann's interpretations of his excavations at Hisarlik, one of many that appeared in Schliemann's lifetime. This is one of the more vitriolic of these attacks, which came chiefly from Germany. Boetticher (also spelled Bötticher) claimed that Schliemann had got it all wrong and that Hisarlik was not the Homeric city of Troy. According to Boetticher, it was not a city at all, but a cremation cemetery or "fire-necropolis." The remains of buildings and walls were used in the rites of the dead; the large storage jars and pithoi were containers for burials or cremated human remains; pottery and other small finds were grave goods; and the signs of burning was evidence only for mortuary ritual. Any evidence that the site was used for habitation was either misunderstanding of the remains by Schliemann, or even worse, deliberate falsification of the plans and documents by Schliemann and his associates.

Boetticher's accusations resulted in a conference organized by Schliemann at Hisarlik in December of 1889 intended to settle the dispute (Trail 1995: 282-285). Schliemann was vindicated and Boetticher's claims were dismissed (as they are today). The essays in this pamphlet were published after Boetticher returned from the conference in order to repudiate the conclusions of the conference that were published in the form of a "protocol," that is itself published in the *Bericht* (1891 in this catalogue) and by Charles Normand in 1892 (see below).

Calder, W.M. 1972. "Schliemann on Schliemann: A Study in the use of Sources." *Greek, Roman and byzantine Studies* 13:335–53.

In this ground-breaking article William Calder ushered in a new era of scholarship that brought to light details about Schliemann's life and work based on a close examination of Schliemann's unpublished writings, such as the diaries, notebooks, and letters in the Gennadius library in Athens. Calder, along with William Easton and David Traill, created an entirely new interest in Schliemann, and Calder's original examination of Schliemann's papers has contributed significantly to the available stock of biographical information about the man. Calder and his colleagues, however, have sometimes been accused of being on something of a vendetta to discredit Schliemann and to blacken his reputation (e.g., Witte 1990; Demakopoulou 1990, *passim*). This new scholarship is nevertheless of great importance, even if some of the more dramatic claims concerning Schliemann's activities on archaeological sites, such as salting the excavations or faking antiquities, go too far (e.g., Runnels 1997).

Calder, W.M., and D.A. Traill, eds. 1986. *Myth, Scandal, and History: The Heinrich Schliemann controversy and a first edition of the Mycenaean Diary*. Detroit: Wayne State University Press.

This important collection of papers is edited by two of the preeminent scholars of Heinrich Schliemann. The papers were originally given at a conference and they cover a wide range of topics, but the subtitle betrays its central purpose. The "controversy" of the title is the result of the efforts by the editors, and Donald Easton, to prove that Schliemann salted his sites, faked antiquities, and falsified his excavation reports. The editors, who wrote most of the text, and two other authors, are hostile to Schliemann, and readers should beware of a certain tendentiousness to this collection of articles.

Ceram, C.W. 1951. *Gods, Graves, & Scholars: The Story of Archaeology.*

New York: Knopf.

This very popular book for general readers was published first in German in 1949 and then had a long life in English translation. It is still in print today. It belongs to the hagiographical literature on Schliemann. Two chapters are devoted to Schliemann and his work, with glowing accounts of his life and adventures embellished with long passages taken from Schliemann's own writings. Ceram's breathless romantic style is no longer in vogue today, and Ceram was not writing a serious history of archaeology. It can be read today in order to form an idea of how strong Schliemann's reputation as a pioneer in the field of archaeology was 50 years after his death. It is also an example of the treatment of Schliemann in archaeological textbooks in the middle of the 20th century. It is the sort of thing I encountered as a student, and if my memory serves, it was the widely accepted view of Schliemann in the decades before the new scholarship by Calder and Traill in the 1970s and after.

Daniel, G.E. 1950. *A Hundred Years of Archaeology*. London: Duckworth.

Daniel's book is one of a series of studies on the history of archaeology published during the middle of the 20th century that touch upon Schliemann's contributions to the growth and development of archaeology. Daniel traces the origins of archaeology back to the Renaissance, but he rather generously acknowledges the significance and originality of Schliemann's contribution to the science as a whole, emphasizing his practical approach to fieldwork and excavation as a way to supplement knowledge derived from texts, something that was relatively rare, if not unique to Schliemann, even in the third quarter of the 19th century.

Daniel, Glyn. 1981. *A Short History of Archaeology*. London: Thames and Hudson.

This one-volume introduction to the history of archaeology is well illustrated and written and is perhaps the best book to read if one has limited time. Because it covers the entire field, unlike McDonald and Fitton, who write about the Greek Bronze Age, the coverage given to individual archaeologists is understandably limited. Daniel was also unable to take advantage of the new scholarship on Schliemann that was just becoming available at the end of the 1970s.

David, B.R., and R. Sapirstein. 1996. "Illustrators and Illustrations in Mark Twain's first American editions." in B.F. Fishkin, ed., *The innocents Abroad*. The Oxford Mark Twain. Oxford: oxford University Press, pp. 23–26.

This is an interesting, and frustratingly short, essay on the use of illustrations in Victorian books. The authors describe the role of large, thick, and heavily-illustrated books for family home entertainment in the era before television and cinema. This aspect of 19th century publishing was not lost on Schliemann, who took a keen interest in the visual presentation of his archaeological discoveries, and the large format, richly-illustrated books such as *Mycenae* (1878) were aimed at the largest possible readership. Schliemann shared the same interest in marketing his books to the general public that is exhibited by Mark Twain, who established his own publishing company to produce and distribute his books.

Schliemann was aware of the force of public opinion in determining the reception of new finds among scholars and savants. Although his main goal was the acceptance of his finds by scholars, his articles in newspapers and periodicals were intended to make his discoveries as widely known as possible and to boost his reputation in the public eye. This strategy made use of the illustrated book then in vogue in Europe and America to popularize his discoveries, and this attention to the mass media is yet another innovative characteristic of the man.

De la Fuente, Maria. 1973. *Schliemann e la nuova archeologia*. Rome: Cremonese.

This is an assessment of Schliemann's archaeological activity from the point of view of the New Archaeology, as it was known in the 1960s and 1970s. I have included this work in order to balance the list of secondary sources in Greek, English, and German. I have not systematically reviewed the literature of the last 25 years in European or other languages, but I suspect that this literature is substantial and that this may be taken as a typical example.

Demakopoulou, Katie, ed. 1990. *Troy, Mycenae, Tiryns, Orchomenos: Heinrich Schliemann: The 100th Anniversary of his Death*. Athens: Greek Ministry of culture and German Ministry of Culture.

This important set of essays and catalogue document an exhibition that traveled from berlin to Athens in 1990 to mark the centennial of Schliemann's death. The authors of the catalogue are clearly not inclined to accept all of the charges of Calder and Traill in connection with Schliemann's archaeological activities, and thus it is good to read the articles in this publication as something of a balance to the flood of criticism that has engulfed Schliemann's reputation in the last 20 years. The photographs of objects found in Schliemann's major excavations are especially valuable. This book has a large and very useful bibliography and the essays are by a wide variety of contributors. Together they make an important contribution to the growing bibliography on Schliemann.

Duel, Leo. 1977. *Memoirs of Heinrich Schliemann: A Documentary Portrait Drawn from His Autobiographical Writings, Letters, and Excavation Reports.* New York: Harper and Row.

I have included this book here because it brings together large numbers of original documents to let Schliemann "speak for himself." Duel is dissatisfied with the general run of biographies and has assembled passages from Schliemann's many autobiographical writings to tell his story. It is a very useful source of information for the beginning student, and it represents an early attempt at a thoroughly documented biography of Schliemann. It still relies in an overly uncritical manner on Schliemann's own writings, something that is no longer accepted.

Fitton, J. Lesley. 1995. *The Discovery of the Greek Bronze Age.* London: British Museum.

This scholarly history of the discovery of the Greek Bronze Age is well illustrated and readily accessible to the general reader. From my point of view, the strongest feature of the book is the balanced assessment of Schliemann and his work at Troy and Mycenae. This is the best account of the subject currently available, with the exception of William McDonald's *progress into the past.*

Hermann, Joachim, ed. 1992. *Heinrich Schliemann: grundlagen und ergebnisse Moderner Archäologie 100 Jahre nach Schliemanns Tod.* Berlin: Akademie-Verlag.

This study of Schliemann's contribution to archaeology has numerous scholarly papers in English and German divided into sections on Schliemann's life and excavations, with a long section on recent scholarship on Aegean prehistory in areas researched by Schliemann. Many of the papers present new archival data, such as the correspondence between Schliemann and Dörpfeld, Schuchhardt, and Gladstone, as well as statements by critics, such as Donald F. Easton's paper, "Was Schliemann a liar?" There is a wealth of scholarly detail in this book, enough to give the reader a sense of the field of Schliemann studies as it stood in the early 1990s. The fact that there are 47 papers, some by multiple authors from many different countries, is a testament by itself to the vigorous interest in Schliemann and his work 100 years after his death.

Korres, George, Styl. 1974. Βιβλιογρία Ἐρρίκου Σκῆμαν.

Βιβιοθήκη τῆς ἐν Ἀθήναις Ἀρχαιολογικῆς 78. Athens: Archaeological Society.

This is the most important bibliographical contribution to Schliemann's writings and publications of which I am aware. It was issued in printed wrappers by the Archaeological Society of Athens, a private institution, in 1974 and is now out of print and largely unavailable. This is a great pity. Its usefulness for many scholars and general readers is limited by the lack of a translation. Despite these unfortunate limitations, professor Korres' bibliography is the best there is, and it is an indispensable starting place for anyone interested in the writings of Heinrich and Sophia Schliemann. The book has 200 printed pages and 16 photographic plates (with illustrations of Heinrich and Sophia, examples of Schliemann's holographic manuscripts, and views of the Iliou Melathron and the Schliemann mausoleum in Athens).

After a short introduction, the book is divided into three sections. The first section lists the works written by the Schliemanns from 1867 to 1892 and has 296 numbered entries. Each of the numbered items contains more than one letter or article, so the number of publications is greater than that indicated by the catalogue numbers. Along with articles in newspapers and journals, all of Schliemann's books are listed, including the autobiography (*Selbstbiographie*), with a list of reprints published before 1974. Contemporary reviews are listed under the entry for each book, which is a useful feature permitting the reader to track the scholarly and public reaction to the publication of Schliemann's books.

The second section lists publications connected with the Schliemanns by other authors from 1870 to 1974. These publications are extremely varied. The entries are numbered from 297 to 2222 and are collected under a large number of heads ranging from the excavations at Troy and the question of Homeric Troy to the excavations at Mycenae, Orchomenos, Tiryns, and other sites. A number of newspaper articles by Sophia Schliemann are included in this section, as are the obituaries and other notices that flooded the press after Schliemann's death in December 1890, and which are itemized on a daily basis through December 1890 to March 1891 (entries numbered 1211 to 1822). Also included in this section are biographies of Schliemann (e.g., Payne, *The gold of Troy*), collections of his letters (e.g., Meyer, *Briefe*), romantic novels about Heinrich and Sophia (e.g., Irving Stone, *The Greek passion*), and a wide range of specialized publications by Aegean prehistorians that touch upon Schliemann, his excavations, or the history of archaeology (e.g., William McDonald, *progress into the past*).

The third section contains additions to the main sections that were evidently added after the rest of the text had been completed. There are 15 entries for the first section and 105 entries for the second section. A final small section, not numbered as part of the main body of the text, lists publications, chiefly reviews and newspaper articles, that were found in one of the "Scrapbooks" in the Schliemann archive at the Gennadius library but which lack sufficient bibliographic detail to completely identify their sources. There are also two indices, one for authors and the other for the titles of periodicals and newspapers.

Korres, George Styl. 1975–1976. "Les inscriptions d'Iliou Mélathron." *Evphrosyne: Revista de Filologia Clássica* NS 7:153–67.

This article is an interesting study that contributes to the small body of studies of Schliemann as an archaeologist and classical scholar. Professor Korres discusses the inscriptions, all drawn from classical authors, that decorate the interior of the large neo-classical private home of the Schliemanns (the Iliou Melathron) in Athens.

Korres, George Styl. [n.d., ca. 1990] *Heinrich Schliemann: Ein Leben für die Wissenschaft: Beiträge zur Biographie.* Berlin: Nicolai.

In this short but very useful work, Korres offers a contribution toward the biographical literature of Schliemann. It was prepared at the time of the centennial observances to mark the death of Schliemann, and it includes a thoughtful evaluation of Schliemann's contributions to archaeology, a useful bibliography, and a large number of high-quality black and white photographs that show, among many interesting things, the furniture from the Iliou Melathron (Schliemann's house in Athens) and his family mausoleum in the first cemetery in Athens. According to professor Korres, Schliemann's contributions to archaeology were in the area of excavation practice or "shovel research." Among the things for which he can be praised were the rapid and full publication of his major excavations. Even if he sometimes left smaller projects incompletely published he is still a model to be emulated by modern archaeologists. Korres also notes, among other matters, Schliemann's use of textual sources, collaboration with staff and specialist colleagues, and his interdisciplinary approach to fieldwork.

Lascarides, A.C. 1977. *The Search for Troy: An exhibit prepared and Described by A.C. Lascarides*. Bloomington: Lilly Library of Indiana University.

This slender volume is a catalogue published to accompany the exhibit of books, papers, and photographs connected with Troy that was mounted at the Lilly Rare Book Library at Indiana University (Bloomington). It is out of print and very scarce today, but extremely interesting and useful for the Schliemann scholar. In the section on Schliemann's activities at Troy his Trojan books are described in some detail, and Lascarides provides an insightful overview of Schliemann's activities at Troy and his relations with Clavert and his critics. Lascarides's comments on the making of the rare photographic *Atlas* of Trojan antiquities are particularly valuable and interesting. Lascarides was a noted bibliophile and book collector, and I have relied heavily on his catalogue while preparing this handlist.

Lilly, Eli, ed. 1961. *Schliemann in Indianapolis*. Indianapolis: Indiana Historical Society.

This little-known gem can be read with pleasure by any Schliemann enthusiast. Schliemann's time in Indianapolis has been neglected by many biographers, and it was left to the Indianapolis native, amateur archaeologist, and philanthropist Eli Lilly to investigate the available evidence and compile this entertaining short study. The Schliemann letters published here for the first time throw much light on Schliemann's day-to-day activities. He was in Indianapolis to obtain a divorce from his Russian wife Katerina, and many letters relate to this activity. But here, too, we find the indefatigable Schliemann rising early, attending to business, speculating in real estate, and writing to numerous correspondents in a variety of languages on an astonishing range of topics, which range from the authenticity of the Arabian Nights manuscripts to Schliemann's search for an arranged marriage with a Greek woman. One can hardly think of a more revealing collection of documents, and it is much to be regretted that a similar volume has not been prepared to document Schliemann's daily life in Paris or Athens. This book has not been reprinted, but it is widely available on the used book market today.

Ludwig, Emil. 1931. *Schliemann: The Story of a Gold-Seeker*. Translated from German by D.F. Tait. Boston: Little, Brown and Company.

This is an early and not particularly uncritical biography of Schliemann, which is included here in order to give the curious reader a taste for the type of biography that predominated in the first 75 years after Schliemann's death. There is also an English edition of this book published under the title of *Schliemann of Troy: The Story of a Goldseeker* (London and New York: G.P. Putnam's Sons) with an introduction by Sir Arthur Evans and illustrations not found in the American edition.

In the preface to the American edition Ludwig informs us that he was asked to do this biography by Sophia Schliemann and had access to all of Schliemann's diaries and papers, some 20,000 items, then in her possession. He tells us that he transcribed "as little as possible" and did not depart "from my principle never to research but always merely to describe" (p. vii). He admits that some research into this mass of papers was necessary and goes on to describe Schliemann as a "monomaniacal" and "mythomaniacal" personality whose life story is "a great human romance, and would be incredible were not every page supported by documentary evidence." Ludwig, however, portrays Schliemann in narrow terms as "a gold seeker," and this, when combined with the uncritical use of Schliemann's writings, is indeed incredible. It is well illustrated, however, and is still quite readable today.

MacDonald, William A. 1967. *Progress into the past: The Re-Discovery of*

Mycenaean civilization. New York: Macmillan.

Schliemann features prominently in this history of Aegean prehistory by one of the leading Aegean prehistorians of his day. McDonald's book is still available as a paperback second edition. McDonald devotes two chapters to Schliemann. The book's greatest strength, however, is its coverage of the field from earliest times until the end of the 1960s, which is all the more valuable because the author knew many of the people in the field and was an active participant in many projects. He spoke from experience and from the perspective of a specialist in the field. Lesley Fitton's book on the same topic is likely to be read more today because it updates the story to the mid 1990s, but this important and pioneering history of the field should not be neglected.

Meyer, Ernst. 1936. *Briefe von Heinrich Schliemann: Gesammelt und mit einer Einleitung hrsg. Von E. Meyer. Geleitwort von W. Dörpfeld.* Berlin: W. de Gruyter.

This is a collection of Schliemann's original letters on many subjects. It is an important source of original documents for those who wish to dig deeper into Schliemann's life and work and who cannot travel to Athens to examine the original archive in the Gennadius library.

Normand, Charles. No date [ca. 1892]. *La Troie d'Homère.* Paris: L'Ami des monuments et des Arts.

This rather rare title was issued in a limited edition (limitation not stipulated, but my copy is number 34) of 114 numbered pages and 29 plates loose in a portfolio with brown printed card covers, silk ties, and a cloth spine. Its importance is in the contemporary photographs taken by Normand of the Trojan antiquities in their display cases in berlin and of the excavations Hisarlik, which Norman visited in 1890. An appreciation of Schliemann's generosity for expending his fortune on the study of archaeology is followed by Normand's account of his trip to the Troad to photograph the excavations at Hisarlik and a discussion of the architecture and small finds from each level.

The photographs taken of the berlin exhibits have a special charm: one sees pithoi mounted on elaborate wooden plinths and supported by wrought iron strapwork and glass vitirines crammed, as was the Victorian custom, with small finds in no particular order. One of the wooden plinths supporting a pithos is encrusted with spindle whorls and stone tools such as querns. The small finds are screened by what looks like chicken wire. A skull is perched, rather precariously one thinks, on a glass vitrine.

Payne, Robert. 1959. *The Gold of Troy: The Story of Heinrich Schliemann and the Buried Cities of Ancient Greece.* New York: Funk and Wagnalls.

This is another of the uncritical biographies that dominated the market in the first half of the 20th century. Badly out of date, it is nevertheless a very readable if highly romanticized biography based on Schliemann's autobiographies and the work of Ludwig (see above). Payne's book describes Schliemann, late in life, as "an old man mad for gold" who believed only in Homer. These misleading oversimplifications set the tone for the whole book. It has been reprinted often and is the most readily available of the older Schliemann biographies.

Runnels, Curtis. 1997. "Review of *Schliemann of Troy: Treasure and Deceit.*" *Journal of field Archaeology* 24:125–30.

This review of Traill's biography (see below) is an example of the scholarly reaction to the book. It challenges some of Traill's conclusions about Schliemann's deceptive practices in archaeology. I believe my perspective to be reasonably representative of the majority opinion of professional archaeologists who specialize in Aegean prehistory.

Traill impugns Schliemann's reliability as an archaeologist and implies that his mendacity in business and in his private life may have carried over into his excavations and publications. I take a different view, arguing that there is little concrete evidence to support accusations that Schliemann salted sites, faked antiquities, or falsified archaeological records. This is a significant debate because Schliemann excavated some of the most important sites in the region, and if Schliemann's excavation reports cannot be trusted the negative impact on Aegean prehistory would be difficult to calculate. Research at the key Aegean sites has built upon Schliemann's research for more than 100 years and the assumption has always been that the facts in these reports can be trusted. In my opinion, David Traill, who is not an archaeologist, does not make a convincing case for fraud in Schliemann's archaeological activities.

Samuel, Alan e. 1966. *The Mycenaeans in History.* Englewood cliffs, NJ:

Prentice-Hall.

This slender volume, now out of print, is an example of the state of the field as it was in the 1960s, long after Schliemann's death but before the revisionist history of Schliemann's career in the 1970s. It is a useful little book for gauging professional opinion as it stood in the middle of the last century.

Schanpp, Alain. 1996. *The Discovery of the past.* London: British Museum Press.

This very useful history of archaeology can be placed alongside Trigger's *History of Archaeological Thought* (see below) as a major contribution to this field.t covers much the same ground as Trigger or Glyn Daniel but from a continental European, specifically French, perspective. Schnapp is a classical archaeologist, not a prehistorian like Trigger and Daniel, and this has influenced his choice of persons and topics to include in his history. Schliemann plays no part here, not so much because he failed to contribute to the development of the field but more as a result of the steady erosion of Schliemann's reputation by the revisionist scholarship of the 1970s and 1980s.

Schuchhardt, Carl. 1890. *Schliemann's Ausgrabungen in Troja, Tiryns, Mykenae, Orchomenos, Ithaka im Lichte der heutigen Wissenschaft. Leipzig*: F.A. Brockhaus [2nd printing 1891].

This is the first edition of Schuchhardt's comprehensive study of Schliemann's excavations. It was prepared during Schliemann's lifetime, and Schliemann read and approved the text (somewhat reluctantly) before his untimely death in December 1890. Schuchhardt summarizes Schliemann's major excavations and advances his own hypotheses. He did much to help clear up some of the confusion and contradictions that are found in Schliemann's writings, which were, as we know, written hastily near the time of the excavations.

Schuchhardt, Carl. 1891. *Schliemann's excavations: An Archaeological and Historical Study.* Translated by Eugénie Sellers. With an appendix on the recent discoveries at Hissarlik by Dr. Schliemann and Dr. Dörpfeld, and an introduction by Walter leaf. Seven maps and plans, 2 portraits

(Schliemann and Sophie), and 297 woodcuts. [xvi] + 348 pp. London and New York: Macmillan.

This book is an essential element of any serious study of Schliemann and his work. He pulls together in one volume all of the important finds and discusses them in a single connected narrative of great clarity and usefulness to those coming to these sites and Schliemann's work for the first time. There is a short biography of Schliemann at the beginning with some interesting details about his home life based on Schuchhardt's personal observations, such as Schliemann's habit of constantly receiving visitors at this Athens home, where he was often found reading a classical text with a pile of stock exchange reports by his side. There is also a useful translation of the last of Schliemann's reports on the excavations at Troy, which otherwise appeared only in German in the *Bericht* (1891). The introduction by Walter leaf serves as a useful corrective to some of Schuchhardt's conclusions and is more likely to find favor with Aegean prehistorians than some of the views of Schuchhardt or of Schliemann. Schuchhardt's text was reprinted by Benjamin Blom, New York, 1971 and Ares, New York, 1974; Avenel, New York, 1979 with a new foreword by Ellen N. Davis.

Secord, J.A. 2000. *Victorian Sensation*. Chicago and London: University of Chicago Press.

This recent book is a contribution to the history of science that traces the story of the Robert chamber's *The Natural History of Creation*. It has nothing to do with Heinrich Schliemann, but it has an excellent, and very detailed, discussion of book publishing in Victorian times. There is much here on the aesthetics, technology, economics, and social history connected with publishing in this era, which was a revolutionary time in the history of printing. The steam press, for instance, made it possible to produce larger numbers of copies of books very quickly, just as the steam train system that sprang up in Europe and America in the middle of the 19th century made the distribution of books easier. As the economy of scale made possible by the new steam technology drove down prices, rising literacy and spreading education made significant contributions to the pool of potential readers. By the time that Schliemann began to publish in archaeology in 1869, the conditions were in place to reach a large audience with articles in newspapers and periodicals, and of course with books. Schliemann was arguably among the first archaeologists to make maximum use of new technologies in his publishing ventures. He was not the first: Austen Henrylayard's enormously popular books describing his adventures in the Near east and his excavations at Nineveh and Nimroud, which began to appear in 1849, must be accounted as among the first great popular successes in archaeology.

Siebler, Michael. 1990. *Troia-Homer-Schliemann: Mythos und Wahrheit.* Mainz: Von Zabern.

This is a well-illustrated account of Schliemann's excavations and research at Troy written to coincide with the centennial of Schliemann's death and to describe some of the results of the first season of the new excavations at Troy by a team from the University of Tübingen. The photographs and plans are of excellent quality, and there is a good bibliography on Schliemann and Troy that includes most significant items to the time of publication.

Stone, Irving. 1975. *The Greek passion.* New York: garden city.

At least one example of the sort of romantic historical novel about Heinrich and Sophia Schliemann should find its way onto every reading list. Stone's narrative, while drawn from Schliemann's own writings, cannot be taken seriously as biography. Neither is it, in my opinion, a particularly good novel.

Traill, David A. 1993. *Excavating Schliemann: collected papers on Schliemann.* Atlanta: Scholars Press.

David Traill is an authority on the life of Heinrich Schliemann, and his important biography (see next item) is the most important life of Schliemann yet written. Traill has been working on the Schliemann papers for more than 25 years and this volume of collected papers brings together in one handy volume all of Traill's major publications on this subject. This book is somewhat difficult to find in libraries or in the used book market, but the articles it reprints are even more difficult to track down.

Traill, David A. 1995. *Schliemann of Troy: Treasure and Deceit.* New York: St. Martins.

This is the only documented and comprehensive biography of Schliemann, and it is the essential starting place for anyone interested in his life. The author has devoted decades of research to the writing of this biography, and the reader and reviewer is certain to be impressed by the impressive marshalling of sources and detail in this monumental work. It is also tendentious in the most negative sense. Traill sets out to attack Schliemann's reliability as an archaeologist by arguing for a pattern of deceptive practices in connection with all of his excavations. According to Traill, Schliemann salted the Shaft graves at Mycenae with artifacts, including faked antiquities (among which Traill includes the famous golden Mask of Agamemnon), and forged the discovery of Priam's Treasure at Troy, which Traill considers to be not a real hoard but a fraud made up from artifacts collected from many sites in the Troad. If these charges are true it would be a serious blow to Mycenaean and Trojan archaeology in particular and Aegean prehistory in general as it would call into question almost all of the finds made by Schliemann in his excavations. These finds have been accepted as genuine from the beginning and more than 100 years' worth of writing about Bronze Age art and archaeology has been based on this assumption. If Traill is proven correct by future research it would be necessary, in the most brutal literal sense, to throw out our textbooks and start all over again. It should be noted that the majority of Aegean pre-historians who are qualified to have an opinion do not accept the substance of Traill's accusations.

Trigger, b. 1989. *A History of Archaeological Thought.* Cambridge:

Cambridge University Press.

This is the best available history of archaeology. Trigger discusses Schliemann's contribution to the founding of archaeology, although Schliemann does not figure greatly in this work. Trigger traces the development of archaeology from Medieval times to the present day with a special emphasis on the contributions of European thought from the Renaissance and the enlightenment to the development of archaeology as a discipline. In this scheme Schliemann is credited with some contribution to the furtherance of fieldwork and excavation, but Trigger evidently considers his theoretical contribution to be negligible.

Uckehurst, Frederick, C. Malley, E. Penner, and Paul Spindler, 1901.

Methode Schliemann—Englisch. Stuttgart: Wilhelm Violet.

This book is not by Schliemann or about his archaeological work, but I wanted to include it in this handlist because it is very rare, unusual, and interesting. This work purports to be "The Natural Manner for learning foreign languages after the Model of Heinrich Schliemann." it was published as a loose portfolio in a printed cloth box (the printed cloth binding is a red, blue, and white pictorial design resembling late Art Nouveaux or early Art Deco). I examined the third edition or printing, which has a laid-in printed sheet referring to the "duration of the War" possibly dating this printing to c. 1914. Inside the covers of the binding are printed advertisements for versions of this work in English, French, Italian, and Spanish.

The portfolio contains a pamphlet of 12 pages in brown wrappers followed by 22 separate parts, with 70 lessons, for a total of 544 pages of texts, jokes, and conversations in English, with transliterations into phonetic notation and with German translations. The parts have continuous pagination. The first part (priced at 1 Mark) has light green wrappers, a portrait of Heinrich Schliemann on the front wrapper, and a reproduction of a letter from Sophie Schliemann (in German) printed on the verso of the front wrapper. There is a color map of London, a color plate of English money, black and white maps of London as part of an exercise in finding one's way around town, a typical restaurant menu in English with a German translation, and a railway guide. Much of the content consists of reading and conversation exercises that are said to be based on the method Schliemann used to learn foreign languages, which is described in the autobiographical sketches that Schliemann provided for his publications. A pleasant feature is the inclusion in each part of "typical" English jokes from the early 20th century. An example: Miss Green: "I have never been able to get a good photograph of my face." Miss White: "Allow me to congratulate you." The last part concludes with a number of useful tables including a list of Americanisms, a chronological summary of English history and literature, and various indices.

von Burg, Katerina. 1987. *Heinrich Schliemann: for gold or glory*. Kings Langley, united Kingdom: Windsor.

This biography is difficult to understand. It is not fully documented, as is Traill's biography, nor can it be described as scholarly and comprehensive. It is nothing more than a vitriolic *ad hominem* attack on the person of Heinrich Schliemann by an author who clearly loathes her subject. One wonders why it was written. If nothing else, it is an example of the passion that Schliemann can excite. It certainly stands as a corrective to the undisciplined and uncritical hagiographical writings of early authors, for example, Ludwig and Payne, who more or less accepted at face value Schliemann's autobiographical accounts.

Wace, Alan J.B., and Frank H. Stubbings. 1962. *A Companion to Homer*. London: Macmillan.

This edited volume is, sadly, out of print. Conceived as the archaeological handbook to accompany the serious student of the Aegean bronze Age, this collection of papers on Homer's poems, the geography of Greece, Aegean languages, and the history of Homeric archaeology, with detailed chapters on the religion, burial customs, and material culture of the Aegean world is a gold mine of information and insight. Of particular value here is the chapter on the "History of Homeric Archaeology" by Alan Wace, which contains a very useful account of Schliemann's archaeological career as seen by his English successor in the excavation of Mycenae.

Weber, Shirley H., ed. 1942. *Schliemann's first Visit to America 1850–1851*. Gennadeion Monographs 2. Cambridge: Harvard University Press. Published for the American School of classical Studies at Athens.

The contents of this important collection of extracts from Schliemann's travel diaries that are found in the Schliemann archive in the Gennadius library at Athens are not archaeological in nature. Weber translates and publishes the diaries of Schliemann's travels in America to add to the growing documentation of Schliemann's life. It is of course invaluable, but it does not add anything to our understanding of his archaeological activities as this journey took place before Schliemann began his archaeological career. It makes great reading, however, and i have included it here because it represents one of the still relatively few contributions to the publication of Schliemann's letters, diaries, and unpublished writings.

Witte, R. 1990. "Schliemann's importance for Modern Archaeology." in K. Demakopoulou, ed., Troy, Mycenae, Tiryns, and Orchomenos. Athens: Ministry of culture and German Ministry of culture, pp. 32–47.

This short but very interesting essay is a contribution to the growing appreciation of Schliemann's innovations in archaeological method and theory. Witte takes issue with the revisionist group of Schliemann scholars as exemplified by Calder and Traill. He lists Schliemann's many contributions to archaeology, which include the use of trial trenches, problem orientation, research design, and rapid publication. Any serious consideration of these points should give pause to Schliemann's critics.

SHORT TITLE LIST
IN ALPHABETICAL ORDER

<u>Troy and its Remains</u>

Table of Contents